Migrating Large-Scale Services to the Cloud

Eric Passmore

Apress®

Migrating Large-Scale Services to the Cloud

Eric Passmore
Bellevue, WA, USA

ISBN-13 (pbk): 978-1-4842-1872-3   ISBN-13 (electronic): 978-1-4842-1873-0
DOI 10.1007/978-1-4842-1873-0

Library of Congress Control Number: 2016942540

Managing Director: Welmoed Spahr
Lead Editor: James DeWolf
Development Editor: Douglas Pundick
Editorial Board: Steve Anglin, Pramila Balen, Louise Corrigan, Jim DeWolf, Jonathan Gennick,
    Robert Hutchinson, Celestin Suresh John, James Markham, Susan McDermott,
    Matthew Moodie, Douglas Pundick, Ben Renow-Clarke, Gwenan Spearing
Coordinating Editor: Melissa Maldonado
Copy Editor: Mary Behr
Compositor: SPi Global
Indexer: SPi Global
Artist: SPi Global

Distributed to the book trade worldwide by Springer Science+Business Media New York, 233 Spring Street, 6th Floor, New York, NY 10013. Phone 1-800-SPRINGER, fax (201) 348-4505, e-mail orders-ny@springer-sbm.com, or visit www.springer.com. Apress Media, LLC is a California LLC and the sole member (owner) is Springer Science + Business Media Finance Inc (SSBM Finance Inc). SSBM Finance Inc is a **Delaware** corporation.

For information on translations, please e-mail rights@apress.com, or visit www.apress.com.

Apress and friends of ED books may be purchased in bulk for academic, corporate, or promotional use. eBook versions and licenses are also available for most titles. For more information, reference our Special Bulk Sales–eBook Licensing web page at www.apress.com/bulk-sales.

Any source code or other supplementary materials referenced by the author in this text is available to readers at www.apress.com. For detailed information about how to locate your book's source code, go to www.apress.com/source-code/.

Printed on acid-free paper

To my wonderful family, their endless love left no room for doubt.

Contents at a Glance

Contents

Foreword

Eric and I met for the first time at a DevOps workshop where thought leaders from many large companies came together to discuss our passion: how to make IT organizations more effective and how to support our business stakeholders better. In my role as the Asia Pacific lead for DevOps at Accenture, I talk to many clients about their IT landscape and challenges. Eric's story stands out to me. I was impressed with his approach and his results. He was very open about his successes and failures. This openness comes through in this book as well.

Eric and I share a passion for openness, and we shared our concern that some stories are just a little bit too clean. That is certainly not true in this book. In the first part of this book, Eric tells his story honestly, detailing what worked and what didn't work. What I especially like is his insight that a "recipe" that works in one context might not work in another. This is so very true from my experience as well. In the second part of this book, Eric actually shares his deliverable, the checklist, with the reader. How rare it is that people share their actual deliverables.

It speaks for the DevOps community and Eric that he shares with us his checklist. I will certainly use it myself, and writing this introduction is the least I can do to thank him for sharing his book with the DevOps community. I look forward to talking about Eric's story at Microsoft and sharing his checklist with many of you at DevOps conferences, meetups, and on projects.

Enjoy this book. I am sure you will learn many things from Eric's experience of creating a multi-national, large-scale web platform and his approach to coaching a large organization to improve.

—Mirco Hering
Principal Director at Accenture and the
APAC DevOps and Agile lead for Accenture

About the Author

Eric Passmore is an online media and technology executive working at Microsoft. He has previously held executive roles at AOL and CBS Interactive. During his 20-year career he has served as head of platforms and infrastructure, content management, application development, and online media. Eric has developed real-time systems to power online social activities and demand-based systems to create customized and relevant experiences. He is a co-inventor of a patented system that creates personalized experiences from large volumes of online content. Eric is passionate about creating resilient services. He is a frequent speaker on topics of large-scale cloud services and improved operational practices.

Acknowledgments

I am extremely grateful and in awe of the formal reviewers. Chivas Nambiar, Rob Cummings, and Mirco Hering provided feedback and direction that made this a better book. I am grateful to Chivas for working through every sentence with thoughtfulness and care. He made sure the ideas were clear, and reminded me of the importance of writing a book for the whole team. Rob Cummings pointed out numerous ideas that I had not yet discovered. He tirelessly reminded me not to bury the lede, and therefore he was the instigator of many rewrites. My special thanks go to Mirco Hering. He provided spot-on critiques of the book while inspiring me during the final push.

I would like to thank all of the teams who participated in the huge effort described in this book. People poured their heart and soul into making something better. This passion fueled many discussions. The honest conversations that came from those discussions provided courage to do the right thing and shift to a checklist late in the project. Special thanks to the Quality of Service team; they always looked for the win-win solution that benefited the entire organization, despite immense pressure to deliver.

The staff at Apress was wonderful to work alongside. Thanks to James DeWolf for opening the door and inviting me to write this book. Thanks to Douglas Pundick for sharing all of his experience with me, a first-time book writer. Douglas provided structure and direction when I needed it most. Thanks to Melissa Maldonado for spending time to answer my questions on the tools and templates.

I cannot thank my family enough for granting me the time to work on this book. Their devotion inspired me to hit every deadline. They were my pillar thoughout the process of writing this book, and I would accomplish very little without their love.

Introduction

This is a book with answers. The last chapters contain over 90 checklist items to build resilant cloud services. These checklist items are a guide that will make good teams great. The checklist covers key pre-release tests, deployment, monitoring, alerting, and mitigation. The checklist covers the full lifecycle of a software service's hosted, public cloud infrastructure, and provides a complete picture of what goes into building a successful cloud service.

I know that these checklist items work because they were used on a global project with hundreds of engineers and hundreds of millions of customers. The first half of this book walks through a true and honest account of what happened on this project. This account will make you laugh and cry as you experience the painful failures and surprising successes. Truth be told, the checklist was the last-gasp effort to successfully deliver after a string of failures. To understand why the other methods failed and why the checklist succeeded, you need to walk through the experience of migrating a large-scale service to the cloud.

The first part of this book tells the story of migrating MSN, Microsoft's consumer-facing portal, to Azure. In telling this story, I share what worked, what did not work, and why. The last part of this book explains how to build a resilant cloud service through an extensive checklist. This book should provide both the answers to get you started and the leadership techniques demonstrated by example to see your project through to completion.

CHAPTER 1

The Story of MSN

This book provides a set of checklists to successfully build very large cloud services. The checklists are battle tested. They were used to launch services supporting hundreds of millions of users. The checklists work because they provide the explicit and implicit requirements for building out resilient services in the public cloud. Any team can pick up the checklist today and use it on their projects.

This book is divided into two parts. The first five chapters tell the story of building MSN, Microsoft's consumer-facing portal, from the ground up on Azure, Microsoft's public cloud. It is a riveting story of building something really big in a few months, and it shares both successes and failures. Readers who want the inside story on developing cloud services in large organizations should take a look at Chapters 2-5. Chapters 6, 7, and 8 describe the checklists used to successfully build cloud services. The checklists cover pre-release, deployment, monitoring and alerting, and mitigation. Readers who wish to gain immediate insight on building cloud services should jump straight to the checklist chapters.

Why I Wrote This Book

Software is a dynamic, constantly changing environment, and there are few tools at the organizational level to build high quality software. Technology is enabling changes in consumption patterns, and those changing consumption patterns are disrupting existing business and business models. Many organizations find themselves needing to transform their businesses, and they need technology to enable those changes. Organizations find they need new capabilities to power mobile, social, and real-time experiences, and they need competent technology leaders to make these advancements. This book provides the management techniques and tools to make great technology leaders. It explains two different methods for managing large-scale software development, and provides an explicit 93-point checklist to build resilient cloud services.

© Eric Passmore 2016
E. Passmore, *Migrating Large-Scale Services to the Cloud*,
DOI 10.1007/978-1-4842-1873-0_1

Why Building Software Is so Challenging

Building software is not easy, and leading teams of software developers is challenging. Developing large-scale software in the cloud is a dynamic, constantly changing environment. In a dynamic environment, leaders are faced with new situations where past experience is a poor guide. The following four challenges create this dynamic environment:

- Constantly evolving technology means old ways no longer apply.

- There's pressure to move faster with larger teams.

- There are challenges to getting information in an increasingly complex environment.

- Massive scale amplifies risk.

The Old Ways No Longer Apply

Technology is constantly evolving and changing. Public cloud offerings are very new and different. In the public cloud, new technologies are employed across all aspects of the software development life cycle. The biggest change is shifting away from discrete SQL databases running on expensive hardware and moving to NoSQL datastores run on commodity hardware. Another challenge is adopting public cloud interfaces to automate deployment, perform updates, and route traffic away from under-performing hosts. In the future, containers and orchestration services will again evolve technology and force teams to adapt their software and services.

This creates a challenging environment for technology leaders. Technology leaders have hands-on experience from their time as individual contributors and line managers that may be a decade old. In the intervening years, the technology has undergone a significant set of changes, and the experiences of the leaders may no longer be relevant. In comparison to other professions, the body of knowledge in software changes at a much faster pace. As an example, consider the legal profession. When lawyers start out, they practice in their field and learn the laws and case decisions. By the time they become partners and managers, much of their experiences are still relevant. They need to keep up with the changes that occur, but they do not need to relearn their profession.

Software development is very different from other professions. The changes are so dramatic and happen at such a fast pace that leaders often find themselves unable to function in a hands-on manner. Technology leaders need management techniques and methods for managing complexity and surfacing key decisions agnostic of the underlying technology.

Moving Faster With Bigger Teams

Fortune 500 companies are finding that the multi-year development cycles they once used are not enough to match competition. In addition, online distribution of software has enabled fixes and updates to occur at several intervals after a major release. Today large companies are moving to a yearly cadence of major releases and striving to hit a monthly cadence for updates. Automated updates are becoming the new normal, and the future cadence for releasing software is likely to be even faster.

As companies transform, they are willing to invest in technology. As a result, many companies are bringing technical teams in house and are moving away from outsourced vendors. With this shift, technology leaders are finding they are managing larger teams as vendor management is replaced with in-house talent. Technology leaders have the two-fold challenge of moving faster with larger teams. Addressing these challenges require management techniques to develop new capabilities while controlling risk across a large organization.

Challenges to Getting Information

Technology continues to advance, and today's software developers have advanced tools and software platforms that empower teams to do more. In the public cloud, teams build on top of a sophisticated orchestration layer. Public cloud infrastructure will automatically perform operating system updates, taking hosts out of service, and updating the software. In addition, public cloud software is often built on commodity hardware that is prone to failure. To work around failures, public cloud software can shift load and move services to different hosts.

Working on a sophisticated and dynamic platform brings complexity. Leaders need to amplify the methods and technologies that work while weakening the methods and technologies that fail. Making the decisions on what to amplify requires information and evidence. In a complex environment, that information can be hard to come by as the link between cause and effort is separated by a complex platform. Leaders need to ask the right questions and leverage the power of monitoring and alerting to create an accurate picture of the environment, make better decisions, and provide clear direction.

Massive Scale Amplifies Risk

To meet changing consumption patterns, businesses are finding that information like assortment, pricing, and availability needs to be at the fingertips of the consumer. Extending this information directly to consumers requires stretching back-end systems to handle a significant increase in load. These back-end systems were often built long ago and designed to be less responsive at a smaller scale. Therefore technology leaders need to increase the scale of mission-critical systems and this new level of scale often requires a new architecture.

Building a new system from the ground up carries a lot of risk. Building on new technology requires learning and exploring to figure out the best technologies and processes to utilize. Experimenting and benchmarking are required skills in adopting new technologies. Technology leaders need to drive a structured set of experiments to master new technology at a new scale. These leaders need to standardize the learning from these experiments and spread the learning out through all of the teams. Moving from benchmarking experimental technologies to standardizing those technologies requires a new set of skills that technology leaders need to master.

What's in This Book?

As new demands are placed on technology leaders, they need a set of management techniques and actionable advice. By telling the story of moving MSN to the public cloud, we document the journey and describe the approaches along with a clear-eyed assessment of why the approaches succeeded or failed. In this story, two different management techniques are illustrated to address the challenges and risks of migrating a large-scale service to the public cloud. These management techniques are tools to guide technology leaders and technology teams to successful outcomes.

Chapter 2 describes the risks faced by moving a large workload to the cloud. These risks include learning new technology, working with distributed data, monitoring large systems, engaging teams in news ways of working, integrating complex systems, and reaching the scale to support billions of daily page views. Chapter 3 outlines the three-step process, a management technique that started well but failed in the end. Chapter 4 describes the tension-filled pivot in the last months to an explicit checklist and how that checklist was rolled out across a big team. Chapter 5 reviews what we learned after the launch and captures the key takeaways for teams building cloud services.

The last three chapters reveal the checklist and explain each of the checklist items in detail. Chapter 6 covers pre-release and deployment items. Chapter 7 covers the monitoring and alerting items. Chapter 8 covers the incident mitigation items. These chapters make a great reference, and stand well on their own.

A Broad-Base Approach

This book covers two management techniques. The first management technique is composed of a three-step process that maps out the system, finds the problems, and fixes the problems. This three-step process is essential to managing risk and creating resilient software. The three-step process is a broad-based approach with a heavy focus on exploration and discovery. In the first step, the mapping phase, the teams need to gather four pieces of information about their services. They need to identify dependencies, document the expected workloads, and document the approach to forward and backward compatibility. In the second step, the teams need to identify all possible failures. The teams categorize issues into one of sixteen buckets to score the failures, thereby identifying the most impactful issues. In the last step, the teams identify mitigations and fixes to lessen or remove the business impact.

The three-step process is essentially a set of thought exercises that force teams to think systematically. Through these exercises the teams are able to find and address the greatest weaknesses, thereby creating a resilient system. The wonderful aspect of the three-step process is that it is agnostic to technology and industry. This process may be used in almost any setting across a wide range of disciplines and industries.

As you will see in this book, a broad-based exploration takes time to adapt to the needs of the project. The thoughtful questions designed to expand the thinking of the team can seem odd and out-of-place when compared the immediate realities of day-to-day work. Therefore, some organizations struggle with a broad-based approach and desire a more relatable and explicit approach.

The Checklist Approach

The second management technique is the checklist approach. This technique is well known with proven use in aviation, health care, and computer science. The checklist approach contains an explicit list of practices and procedures to follow for a given activity. The checklist ensures that the proper information is gathered, that information is used to make qualified decisions, and things are left in a good state. Sometimes the checklist will include a goal or expected outcome. As an example, a flight checklist might ask the pilot to climb to 10,000 feet. Sometimes the checklist specifies the method to use. For example, a flight checklist might ask the pilot to broadcast their position every 15 minutes. Therefore checklists contain both expected outcomes and prescribed processes.

Checklists are very specific: they are crafted for a specific technology and a specific work environment in a specific industry. The specific nature of a checklist makes it easy for teams to relate to the work items. At the same time, the specific nature of a checklist prevents it from being used to address a new technology, different industry, or dynamic work environment.

The Case for Checklists

In the end, this book makes the case that checklists are a powerful and useful tool for challenging projects. Checklists have long lost favor with workers, managers, and consultants because their prescriptive nature prevents innovation and improvement. Instead, many practitioners suggest a broad approach using thought exercises combined with experience gained through trial and error. This broad-based approach is captured as part of the three-step approach described in Chapter 3. In the end, the three-step process failed to engage the teams. As a result, teams did not understand how to make their software resilient. In this sense, the three-step approach failed.

In reaction, the leadership team pivoted to a completely different approach. They created an explicit checklist of work items, and assigned the work items to the teams. In the end, it took an explicit list to drive work and get things done. Checklists have had a long history of success, and that history continued with the latest relaunch of MSN.

The Journey

In October of 2014, Microsoft relaunched MSN, their consumer-facing portal (see Figure 1-1). The web site had a new consumer experience, but what you did not see was a completely new, built-from-the-ground-up infrastructure supporting MSN. This book tells the story of rebuilding the infrastructure of MSN on Azure, Microsoft's public cloud.

Figure 1-1. *MSN*

Our journey begins with a business that wants to thrive and grow. MSN as a content portal wanted to grow its audience and increase its engagement with users. MSN is a big business, generating significant revenue for Microsoft, with hundreds of million users across more than 50 international and domestic markets. Making a change in a big business requires big bets. MSN decided to make a bet on premier content from a worldwide collection of top news providers and a fantastic user experience.

Large parts of the infrastructure needed to be overhauled to realize these goals. Sports needed to add leagues, teams, and players while improving live scores. The personal investing site needed updates of stock quotes and tickers along with an improved portfolio manager. Whole new categories of content, such as recipes, chefs, and wine, were added. With each new extension we needed new tools to manage the content and new infrastructure to process and scale to a huge worldwide audience.

To make this a reality over 400 engineers in the United States, Canada, India, and Ireland would be working for over a year to rebuild the site while improving the technical infrastructure. Figure 1-2 shows the locations of the geo-graphically diverse teams and their relative sizes. By any measure, this was a huge engineering effort.

Figure 1-2. *The locations of the MSN Engineering teams*

CHAPTER 2

■ ■ ■

Brave New World

Moving to the public cloud has challenges and carries risks. Managing these risks will be the difference between success and failure. These risks are not always obvious. In this chapter, I call out six different risks: new technology, distributed data, integration, scale, achieving situational awareness, and new human processes. By describing these risks and sharing examples of their impact, I hope you, as a technology leader, will be better equipped to successfully delivery big technology projects.

The story of rebuilding MSN for the public cloud illustrates many of the challenges in dealing with large-scale online systems. Table 2-1 lists the six risks teams face in managing large-scale services in the public cloud.

Table 2-1. *Six Risks in Managing Large-Scale Services in the Public Cloud*

Risk	Description
New technology	Choosing the wrong technology can create bottlenecks, preventing scaling and innovation.
Distributed data	Rugged systems span the globe, so keeping that data synchronized is a challenge.
Integration	Large systems are composed of many parts that need to work together.
Scale	Services that cannot meet customer demand do not serve the business. Global business requires a global footprint.
Achieving situational awareness	Because they lack understanding of all of the moving parts, teams take random walks instead of directed action.
New human processes	Complexity demands that actions be taken in a precise order. Failure to do things the correct way results in outages.

© Eric Passmore 2016
E. Passmore, *Migrating Large-Scale Services to the Cloud*,
DOI 10.1007/978-1-4842-1873-0_2

The adoption of mobile technology, along with online social networks, had enabled changes in consumption patterns. Our customers expect to get their daily news, sports, weather, and finance information quickly and directly. In addition, they want to leverage their online friends to find relevant information and be in the know. Our platform needed to stretch to provide a more targeted and personal experience. We needed to provide information directly to mobile devices, with the fast and rapid cadence our customers expected. We needed a platform that could meet these evolving business needs.

MSN grew up with the Internet. The platform was architected in the early 2000s. The software was designed and created in a time of constrained memory. As a result, the services were limited and could not make full use of memory on newer hardware. Many services lacked redundancy, and the failure of a single piece of hardware could take down critical functionality. As a result, the system frequently suffered outages due to limited capacity, and small outages caused really big problems. During the intervening ten years, some upgrades occurred. The upgrades included moving to the latest version of the operating system, upgrading to new hardware, moving to new datacenters, and automating deployments. Those upgrades were necessary but not enough to meet the evolving needs of the business.

Living with this old infrastructure was like worshiping old gods (see Figure 2-1). We prayed our mobile phones would remain silent. When evil did fall upon us, and the mobile phones went off, we responded with rituals first, and true investigation later.

Figure 2-1. *Worshipping old gods*
(Title: God of Happiness @ Jochi-ji Temple @ Kita-Kamakura. Author: Guilhem Vellut. License: CC By 2.0.)

The engineering teams on pager duty dreaded late night calls. They would spend hours diagnosing long forgotten code pathways and caching logic. During one incident the very first response was restarting all instances of a service. No one seemed to recall why we needed to restart the instances; it was just standard practice. Further investigation revealed there was an old XSLT parser with a memory leak. Large files processed by the old XSLT parser triggered a bug, and the service would run out of memory. Restarting the services was the way we did things.

In addition, it was painful to restore services and data without adequate redundancy. When failures occurred, these systems would go offline, and they needed to be restored manually. Manual restores were tedious and time-consuming.

Incrementally working to modernize our technology was a slow and unsteady process. Each service was at the edge and had no additional capacity. Any changes could upset that balance, create an outage, and force us to roll back. As an example, we rolled out improvements to image processing that enabled our business to process more images faster. Unfortunately, the image storage solution was at its limit, and it could not keep up with the increased image processing speed. All image processing stopped when the image storage became overloaded. So we rolled back our improvements and identified a new work item to scale our image storage solution.

This is just one example. There were many overlapping dependancies, and this back-and-forth of improvement to failure was typical. The knowledge of these dependancies was lost, and that made incremental improvements difficult. One improvement would surface previously unknown dependancies. Those surprise dependancies would surface previously unknown requirements. As a result of those unmet requirements, failures occurred. Every aspect of the system was stretched to its limits. The engineers saw the platform as fragile, and they were afraid it would break with every change. After years of incremental improvements, we needed a new approach.

Reaching our business goals required a new technology stack. From experience we knew the incremental approach was not yielding results, and we decided to build a new platform from the ground up. We were determined to build something that was more reliable and scalable, and had a lower cost of ownership. The incremental approach constrained us by limiting upgrades to the existing components. For example, many components of our system had different storage solutions. Images, video, and documents were all stored in different ways using isolated systems. We really wanted to upgrade the entire storage layer of our platform, and we wanted to use the latest technologies. By building from the ground up we had the freedom to choose any platform and technologies we wanted.

Microsoft's public cloud was appealing due to its ease of onboarding and self-service tools. Developers could spin up services quickly and rapidly build out new features. The public cloud offered more locations and more freedom to ramp up and ramp down compute power to meet business demand. Finally, Microsoft's public cloud had an enormous level of investment, and our teams could ride the wave of innovation by using the public cloud. Azure, Microsoft's public cloud, had technology to speed up development, tooling to lower support costs, the flexibility in capacity, and investment in infrastructure to power the future. For these reasons we decided to build a platform on Azure.

New Technology

Moving from a system and architecture based in the early 2000s to a new system with the latest cloud technology from 2014 was a big change. MSN had huge scale. There were hundreds of millions of users and petabytes of data. Our first task was making sure the cloud could support MSN's workload.

This is a common challenge for organizations moving to the cloud. Technology has changed so much over the last few years, and the cloud stack utilizes a different set of technologies. The biggest change has come in storage. NoSQL storage solutions have become the default storage mechanism of choice. New technology may have advantages but it also has differences. Those differences may not be desirable changes.

Benchmarking

An organization must first decide what technologies to use, and then try out the different solutions. The best solution depends on the workloads it will experience. A variety of analyses must be performed. The most effective analysis comes from benchmark tests with a specific goal. Benchmarks provide empirical evidence that cuts through the theory and supports decisions (see Figure 2-2).

Figure 2-2. *Choose wisely*
(Title: Choose Wisely You Must. Author: Pasi Välkkynen. License: CC By SA 2.0.)

In the first phase of benchmarking it's important to identify how resources like compute, storage, and network will be used. Benchmarking existing systems is a great starting point to determine what resources will be used. In addition, benchmarking needs to include room to grow to meet evolving business needs. As consumption patterns continue to evolve, customers will want a more personalized, real-time experience.

Serving these evolving needs will require more resources. Failing to properly model the size and scope of network, storage, and compute will limit the platform. A limited platform without the ability to grow will make change difficult. Each new change will require expert effort to squeeze out enough new capacity to support the new feature.

At MSN, we did not know how to fit our very large online service into Azure, the Microsoft cloud. It may seem strange that there was no obvious answer. There were no other services of the same large scale, running 24x7, on Azure. Before we created a high-level design, we needed to know exactly how much compute power and storage was required. We also needed to make sure we were able to meet evolving business needs. We looked at our old system as a starting point. We found the peak number of transactions on the old platform. From there we included additional capacity for the new capability of replication, and added twenty percent on the top for headroom.

From this work we created a model for our system. The model was built in spreadsheets. Spreadsheets are a fine tool for building these types of models. Using this model we calculated how much compute, storage, and network we would need. We made sure the model included capacity to serve a more personalized experience delivered directly to mobile devices. In our calculations we did a further breakdown to identify the number of accounts and hosts we would need.

To deliver a more personalized experience we needed to provide our customers with a larger variety of content and provide that content faster. To deliver more content faster we need to deliver an increasing number of documents per second. As we looked through the growth curves, we found some areas that scaled well. There were other areas with limits we could not scale past. One area that had a hard limit was storage. Therefore our calculations told us that writing and reading data would be the most difficult aspect to achieve. Moving to new cloud technologies was a risk, and we did not yet know how to get the scale and performance we needed.

Benchmarking Storage

From our benchmarking we knew we needed 63,000 read and write transactions a second, and we needed to store petabytes of data. A single unit of hardware would not be able to scale to this level while providing the resiliency to failure at a competitive cost. A storage solution of this size, resiliency, and cost was only possible using a distributed storage solution. A distributed storage solution breaks data into distinct groups called shards. The shards are spread across many hosts. When a storage request for a document is received, the distributed storage solution calculates the relevant shard and sends the request to the correct hosts. By spreading the read across many hosts, more compute, storage, and networking resources are available. To perform at peak levels, all of the hosts need to be utilized. To utilize the entire collection of hosts, documents must be distributed so that a same and equal number of requests are sent to each host. Said another way, each host must carry the same load to maximize utilization.

The distribution of requests is an important concept to keep in mind when adding new capacity. Adding new, empty hosts creates new capacity. These new, empty hosts have no documents, and therefore they receive no requests. Fully utilizing the new hosts requires moving documents from existing hosts onto new hosts. This process of moving documents to improve utilization is called rebalancing. Left unchecked, a full rebalancing action will simultaneously transfer many documents and eat up all available network bandwidth. An unchecked rebalancing will slow the distributed storage solution to a virtual stopping point. Therefore, rebalancing is often performed slowly over time while continuing to support existing requests. Rebalancing is complex work. As a result, distributed systems have limits on the storage size and number of transactions they can support for rebalancing.

Out of the box, none of the distributed storage solutions available to our team could manage the size and scale we needed. To meet the needs of our business we would need to build on top of the existing storage solutions. We would need to aggregate together a lot of capacity from individual instances to create a super-sized solution. In addition, to deal with the rebalancing challenge, we would need to configure our system to be big enough from the start. By creating a super-sized solution we could forestall rebalancing for years and buy time to create a proper solution.

Therefore, figuring out how to get 63,000 storage transactions per second was paramount. To be viable, the new platform needed to support our benchmarked goal. There was a lot riding on our choice of storage technologies. The technology team was concerned; a poor choice in technologies or implementation would be fatal to our efforts to rebuild the infrastructure. There were risks from the many unknowns. No one could cite an existing solution that would work. Our volume of user requests, our global reach, and the sheer size of data were much larger than could be supported by the existing solutions. We needed to start benchmarking solutions as a first step and prove success.

We decided to benchmark different storage solutions with different configurations. We set out to benchmark five different types of NoSQL storage technology. Each of the five benchmarks were set up on similar-sized systems hosted in Azure datacenters.

- Public Azure storage
- Two internal Microsoft storage solutions
- Two open source solutions

It was a tedious process to create fake data and scripts to simulate requests. As we ran our tests and stressed the systems, we found the limits and faults in each. Some systems were just plain unreliable. Other systems were not up to the job and could barely do 1/10th of the desired load. We finally settled on Azure Storage as our solution. Azure Storage was consistent and reliable.

We still had a problem, however. We could only get a few thousand read and write transactions a second from a single storage account. We needed ten times that capacity to meet our needs! Azure Storage limited throughput at the account level. These limits were established for good reasons. They were put in place to prevent runaway services and resource hogs from blocking well-behaved services. To move beyond the established storage limits, we would need to aggregate together many storage accounts.

We decided to embrace the scaling limits and build our own service to aggregate together many Azure Storage accounts. We continued to refine and rerun our tests working alongside the internal Microsoft teams to get the best possible performance. Through this rigorous process we learned a lot. In the end, the evidence indicated we would need 42 storage accounts to meet our needs and scale to 63,0000 read and write transactions per second.

Takeaway

It took a team of 12 people three months from the start of benchmarking through the prototyping phase. During the first month, we eliminated three of the five choices due to difficulty of use, lack of scale, and outright bugs. During the second month, we eliminate a forth solution due to lack of query and data management capabilities. In the same month, with our one remaining solution we were able to reach the half-way point in our goal. During the third month of intensive performance tuning, we were able to exceed our goal.

This is a common pattern for benchmarking. Half of the options will be eliminated right away due to obvious problems. Digging into the details of how the technology really works will eliminate more options. In the last phase, it takes repeated experimentation with a single technology to maximize potential. The process of selecting technology and trying options is research, and it will inform the architecture. By the time the teams finish benchmarking they will often already have an architecture in mind. The benchmarking process is both a selection process and a learning process. Had we not done this analysis, our architecture would not have scaled to meet the number of users flooding into our sites. A poor architecture that did not scale would have doomed the project and the entire effort would have been a failure.

Geo-Distributed Data

Today consumers expect services to be up and running every hour of every day. Having a highly available site requires resilient infrastructure to take over in the event of failures. One of the biggest types of failures that can occur is the failure of a datacenter. Datacenters rarely suffer a complete failure. It is more likely that an event in the datacenter impacts your organization's critical components. Events could be a software update to networking equipment, a power outage, or an expired security certificate. During these events, organizations need to utilize their resilient infrastructure and continue to serve their customers.

The risk of having multiple datacenters arises from the requirement to maintain exact replicas of infrastructure with completely different configurations. Replication of data, configuration, and permissions between datacenters are required to keep the datacenters available. In addition to investing in replication, the technical teams need to perform additional engineering to continuously check the health of a datacenter. When a datacenter is not healthy, even more engineering work is needed to route user requests to the healthy datacenters. It all has to work perfectly. Multiple datacenters typically experience the following four failures:

- If the data is not copied correctly, the datacenters will become out of sync.

- False negatives on the health check will result in undetected problems and downtime.

- False positives on the health check will cause disruptive, unneeded failovers.

- Failure to route user requests will result in downtime.

Datacenter Topology

I arrived at Microsoft in late 2010, with a background steeped in Linux. I was eager to learn about the new Windows-based publishing system that supported MSN. I was curious what technology was used to keep the site running with huge surges of traffic. With any large, news-based Internet site, celebrity misdeeds and breaking news stories cause huge surges in users and usage. Many sites and services often have trouble staying up during these big news events. From competitive data I knew that Microsoft had done surprisingly well and continued to reliably serve users.

Since I was now at Microsoft, I had the privilege of reviewing the existing architecture and learning how they had managed so well during these big news events. All of the architecture reviews highlighted a single datacenter design. A single datacenter design was prone to failure. News web sites typically had several datacenters. This redundancy served two purposes. First, the redundancy enabled business continuity and offered the ability to serve users in the event of a datacenter failure. The backup datacenters would take over and continue to serve users. Second, having datacenters spread through the world lessened the physical distance between users and the services they needed. This shorter distance made the responses faster and more reliable. Having more datacenters made the web sites faster.

I was surprised. After several architecture reviews I was no closer to learning the secrets of scaling. I tried a different tactic and asked the head of operations. He informed me there was only one datacenter to serve the MSN home pages. I was flabbergasted. How could one datacenter possibly outperform competitors during these surges in users and usage? The answer was the *static page.*

The static page was an ingenious solution. The static page was created by regularly caching the MSN home page. This static page was stored on a completely separate set of infrastructure and was served to everyone when major incidents occurred or when demands outstripped capacity. This simple solution was the answer to my question.

There was a drawback to this elegant solution. The static page was one page served to everyone. Everyone received the same exact copy of the static page (see Figure 2-3). This prevented personalization of the page. For this reason, the static page stripped out local weather, stock picks, local news, and counts of new e-mails. As the only fallback, the static page was used to mitigate almost every production issue. As a result, the static page was used too often, and too often users would not see their personalized weather, news, and stock picks. The static page was an elegant solution, and when used appropriately bested the competition; however, we needed to do better if we wanted to meet our desired level of reliability.

Figure 2-3. *It would be so much easier if we were all the same*
(Title: Cloning Experiments: Jess Payne. Author: Dan Foy. License: CC By 2.0.)

The old system had many single points of failure, and some key services existed in only one datacenter. Unlike our old system, we wanted our new system to be resilient. Therefore we designed the new system to be *global* from day one and operate out in three separate regions: Asia, the Americas, and Europe. This was an amazing opportunity and at the same time carried a lot of risk. It was hard enough to architect and build a successful solution in one datacenter. We needed to go further and get four datacenters distributed around the world, operating together in unison.

With optimism and energy we rushed forward to embrace this new global architecture and software design. Our large-scale cloud service would start with one master datacenter and four slave datacenters (see Figure 2-4). All the tools and ingestion would write to that master datacenter. The slave datacenters would copy data from the master.

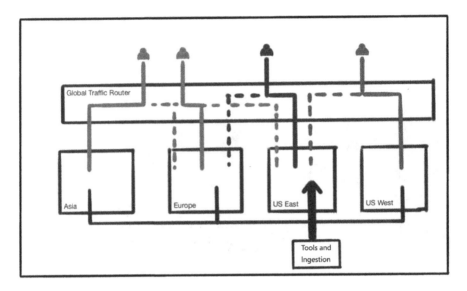

Figure 2-4. *Multiple datacenters*

Routing Around Failure

With some help from Microsoft technology, we sent all of our user traffic through a *global traffic router*. The global traffic router sent all of the user traffic to the best-performing datacenter. If a failure or slowdown occurred in one of the datacenters, the global traffic router would send the user request away from the failed datacenter and onto to the next best datacenter. Our datacenters were not of equal capacity. They were built out to support regional traffic and provide redundancy. Therefore a datacenter with the smallest amount of capacity could not take over from datacenter with the largest capacity. The global traffic router was helped by supported rate limits. These rate limits enabled us to ensure our datacenters were not flooded with too much traffic. It enabled us to effectively spread out load in the event of a datacenter failure. These advanced capabilities went beyond routing of traffic and allowed a more sophisticated response to problems. The global traffic router was like a having a traffic cop direct the flow of vehicles (see Figure 2-5) and open up new lanes in the event of an outage. By sending user requests to the best datacenters, the global traffic router automatically mitigated outages that would have caused an interruption in service. It was a key piece of technology that we found dependable and reliable.

Figure 2-5. *Don't mess with me*
(Title: North Korea - Traffic girl. Author: Roman Harak. License: CC By SA 2.0.)

The global traffic manager was composed of many hosts spread through the world. These hosts existed not in Microsoft datacenters, but in Internet service provider datacenters. Each global traffic manager host operated independently. Together these hosts intercepted all user requests intended for MSN. Once they received the requests they would send them onto the best MSN datacenter. To make this determination, the global traffic manager hosts would frequently ping each MSN datacenter to gauge the responsiveness and free capacity for additional user requests. The most responsive datacenter with free capacity would be chosen as the most desirable MSN datacenter.

Replication of Data

Our staff to manage content was spread across many different countries around the globe. Our business decided to utilize our global workforce and create a more responsive editorial team. By using teams around the globe we could follow the sun and staff a 24x7 editorial team. Teams in Australia could start the day and manage the top English-speaking news events for all other English-speaking markets. The UK would follow, and the US/Canadian team would end our global day. In most systems, content was stored separately in three regions: the Americas, Europe and the Middle East, and Asia Pacific. A separate regional model was not an option. To support a globally unified team the business required a similarly globally unified database.

This was another significant risk: new and updated content needed to reach every datacenter. Breaking news stories needed to be available in minutes to stay competitive and best serve our customers. Unlike the user requests routed by the global traffic manager, there were no good mitigations if a breaking news article was not properly copied to all datacenters. In the event of failures, content around the world could stop updating and become stale. The updates of content had to be flawless to support breaking news. Therefore writing content across datacenters was taken very seriously with a very low tolerance for failure. There was no existing support for global distribution of data, and certainly no solutions that guaranteed to complete the task in seconds. We needed to build our own global replication solution.

Design on the Fly

Do not let your teams be locked into technical decisions. When teams see structural problems, they need to be fixed. Flaws in the basic design of the software are much easier to fix early in the process. Leaders should incorporate new evidence and understanding of the systems to build a rugged and robust cloud service. Teams should be allowed to design on the fly after work has started.

Replicating across geographies is not an easy problem to solve. When building our solution, we made a design mistake that we later had to fix. The first version of the software was built in a single datacenter. The write service, which updated the data, performed a distributed transaction across both the NoSQL store and the Elasticsearch Index. Invalidating caches would have required another distributed update. If we applied this pattern to several datacenters, a single service would be responsible for managing the success, retry, and, if needed, rollback of each update both locally and remote. Successfully executing on that pattern would have required some very complex software logic to manage a distributed transaction. Complex code with transactions often leads to bugs. We needed a new design to simplify our approach.

We decided to change our system. In the new design (see Figure 2-6), the write service needed to write only once to the NoSQL store in the master datacenter. We created a wrapper service around the NoSQL store. This storage service handled all writes into the NoSQL store. We extended the storage service to replicate these updates into the slave datacenters spread around the globe. Each slave datacenter would pull over new updates and changes from the master datacenter. In addition, we again extended the storage service to post a message into a local queue as a notification of updates. The upstream services and data-cache read from the queue and applied the needed updates.

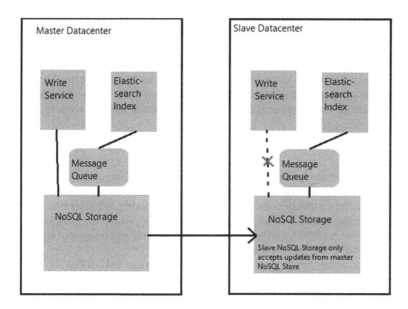

Figure 2-6. *Data replication between datacenters*

This was a much better design pattern. The storage service was the only system aware and able to distinguish between master and slave datacenters. All other services were not aware of the distinction between master and slave datacenters and as a result they were configured, managed, and deployed the same regardless of location. This new design was a huge win for operational support, and the simple pattern improved our chances of writing high-quality software.

Takeaway

Working across multiple datacenters is complicated and requires navigating a complex set of technical choices. It is easy to get off track and stop short of developing a true distributed, multi-datacenter solution. Leaders need to be aware of these very real risks and not take the multi-datacenter approach for granted. The following chapters in this book provide the techniques and strategies that leaders can employ to create platforms with multiple, redundant datacenters.

Integration

One of the biggest risks in building new infrastructure and new systems is integration risk. Services need to talk to each other by exchanging a very precise set of instructions. When services fail to agree on the meaning and intent of messages, failures occur. These issues may be hard to find. Taken separately, each individual component may operate correctly. It is only when these services are combined together that dysfunction is the rule.

Public cloud services are full of integration issues. Public cloud infrastructure is run as a service outside the purview of customers. Customers do not see the infrastructure software updates, the patches, and the hardware updates. Customer services built in the public cloud have self-service tools that make deployment and updating very easy. The ease of updates leads to frequent updates. Each change has a small risk of creating an integration issue. The rapid speed and high frequency of updates in the public cloud lead to a greater pace of change and a greater risk of miscommunication between services.

Simplicity

Working together in a cloud environment requires anticipation of failures. Each component in a system needs to be able to expect and deal with a certain amount of failure. When components cannot deal with failure, they stop working. When a critical component fails, the entire system will fail. For this reason, it is important to create an end-to-end working system early in the development cycle. An end-to-end system will enable teams to find and fix integration issues early.

Finding integration issues between two services is not always an easy thing. The discovery process often bounces back and forth between two different services, collecting data to prove or disprove a hypothesis for the failure in integration. There is hope. Simple services have fewer complexities, making simple services easy to use correctly. Complex services with deep features present many options and are more difficult to use correctly. For this reason, it is often better to have many simple services instead of one big comprehensive service. Specifically, it is best to separate read and write services. Keeping these services separate will ease the risk associated with integration.

Battle Scars

With experience working on large-scale solutions at AOL, CNET, and Microsoft, our teams have fought battles. Along the way, we accumulated battle scars. From time to time they itch, reminding us of past lessons. One of those lessons is how hard it is to make a single service that reads and writes data.

At scale, these services consist of many separate hosts. When updating data, the service may need to perform several actions like writing the document, updating the cache, and logging. Doing this with guarantees requires transactions and locks. This is a very hard problem. Even great engineering teams need a lot of testing and fixes to get everything working right. Experienced teams have learned to hope for the best and plan for the worst. Bugs can cause all sorts of unpleasant problems (see Figure 2-7). If there are bugs in the code, updates will fail with no discernible pattern, the wrong update might get through, content could be accidentally deleted, or the system may lock up and slow to a crawl. Creating read and write services is not an easy task.

Figure 2-7. *Integration gone wrong*
(Title: drive side. Author: Hillel Eflal. License: CC By 2.0.)

Years ago, when working at AOL, I was called during the end-of-the-year holiday break. The most trafficked and most important page was not updating the top stories. The main stories were stale and getting older. It was surprising to have problems because the service had been running for a while. The only recent change was the additional of caching to improve performance. That day the team decided on a workaround by restarting the services and clearing the cache. We continued to investigate, and even I cracked open the code to take a look. We found a lot more than one bug. We found many synchronization issues that would prevent the content from updating. To fully fix the problem, we split the code in two pieces. One half updated the cache. The other half read from the cache.

All of us working on the new MSN publishing system had similar experiences and the same battle scars. We decided it was best to create two separate services. One service was created for reading and the other was created for writing. This separation split the problem and reduced complexity. The split between read and write services enabled new feature development on one service independently of the other service. With this separation, the read service had no data updates and needed no transactions and locking. The hard problem of locking and transactions was encapsulated in the write service. This separation reduced risk and made the overall system better, and it is a pattern recommend for high-scale services.

Takeaway

Integration issues happen when services misinterpret instructions and fail to do the intended work. There are two strategies to help teams manage integration risk. First, teams should build an end-to-end integration environment early in development. Second, teams should simplify their services and consider splitting read and write services.

An end-to-end integration environment will break when there are integration issues. This failure enables teams to find and diagnose issues early. Without the attention on integration issues they are often missed. Therefore an end-to-end environment acts like a flashlight flushing out bugs.

Separating read and write services is a good idea. As system get larger and need to handle higher loads, more complex logic is introduced to cache data and streamline requests. Separating out these two functions eases integration issues and make the system simple to use.

Scale

Big global businesses have lots of users spread around the world. Online services supporting these businesses must meet the thundering herd of customers during peak events. In addition, online services need to be close to the user to have a competitive and responsive experience. Being physically close to users makes better use of networks and cuts down on delays, yielding a faster response. To decrease the physical distance, the services need to be in multiple datacenters in multiple geographic regions.

Switching costs are low for online services. Customers can easy search for and start using competitive services. A service that does not scale will drive users into the arms of competitors. Scaling problems are very often systemic flaws that require redesigning and rebuilding big parts of the infrastructure. Redesigning and rebuilding takes time. Even worse, scaling issues are typically found during the highest periods of usage. Failing during peak usage periods is an opportunity miss that can cause significant harm to the business.

Standards

Services that scale need an architecture that will expand and grow to new levels without sacrificing performance and speed. Bottlenecks in the system will prevent teams from adding more capacity and will prevent services from scaling. To find these bottlenecks, leaders need to set standards and document the desired level of scale. This target can be expressed as two different numbers. By running stress tests against the service and evaluating against these two numbers, leaders can determine if a service is ready to meet demand during peak events:

- **Throughput**: Measure of peak number of requests per second. For example, a service should do 1,000,000 RPS.

- **Latency**: Measure of duration of requests for the slowest percentage of requests. For example, the latency budget for this service is 500ms at 99.9%.

The first metric, throughput, ensures that the service can handle lots of customers at the same time and handle a large volume of requests. The second metric, latency, ensures that the service responds quickly. Services very often slow down as they take on more and more usage. Leaders need to set a high bar and ask the service to support peak volumes of requests without slowing down.

Example

At MSN, once we had targets for services, we started to load the system and run stress tests. We assumed the data from the tests would expose weaknesses that we would find and fix (see Figure 2-8). Instead, a surprising thing happened. We debated and challenged the validity of the data from the stress tests.

Figure 2-8. *Plenty of room on top*
(Title: Just Put It On Top. Author: Christoph Rupprecht. License: CC By SA 2.0.)

At first, all responses were counted. Good and bad responses were included in our analysis. The debate centered around counting errors and including them in our analysis. There were errors that were malformed requests that resulted in errors. There were errors from requests for items that did not exist. Finally, there were internal errors either from bugs in our code or the inability to handle recoverable faults.

Some of the errors caused stack traces. They were expensive and lots of these errors would slow down the system. In addition, requests for non-existent items were treated as errors and they returned very quickly. What we included in our analysis could make the service look artificially slow or artificially fast.

We decided to better classify our errors. The errors from the service would be included and become part of the analysis. The errors from bad and malformed requests would be thrown out and not included in our analysis. To do this, we categorized non-good responses with error codes to account for malformed requests, unauthorized requests, unsupported requests, and requests for deleted content. Going through this process caused the team to come together and align on which requests were valid and which requests should be tossed out from the final measure.

We soon discovered another problem measuring throughput and latency. With the scale and volume of our business, we needed to deploy updates to thousands of hosts across four datacenters. Rolling out changes took time. During that long rollout period, some hosts had the next version of software while other clients had the previous version of software. Having different versions of software created a risk of incompatibilities. We needed to explicitly handle both forward and backward compatibility.

Without standards for forward and backwards compatibility, our services would encounter integration errors, and fail. We needed these standards to keep our services up and running during deployments. We added the following two standards:

- **Correctness**: An explicit definition of a correct response.

- **Compatibility**: An explicit process to deal with forward and backward changes.

  - **Backward compatibility**: New software must handle old schemas.

  - **Forward compatibility**: Old software must handle new schemas.

Having both backward and forward compatibility enables teams to roll out updates independently with a lengthy transition period. With multiple datacenters it is too hard to synchronize the deployment and updates of software. A lengthy transition period is a must when there are multiple datacenters. Therefore meeting the standard of compatibility is the secret that enables teams to scale services across multiple geographic regions.

Takeaway

It is critical that leaders find and fix scaling issues early. This is not easy. It is challenging for leaders to manage all of the technical complexities involved in scaling services while distributing these services in multiple regions.

Instead, leaders should be outcome-focused and set targets for latency and throughput. To make these targets stick, leaders need to work with teams to develop two standards, correctness and compatibility. Setting these targets and establishing these standards will set a high bar and enable teams to deliver geo-distributed services that meet customer demand during peak events.

Achieving Situational Awareness

Online businesses function entirely on the software systems created by their engineering teams. When software crashes or has problems, teams want to know about it right away. Once problems are identified, teams want to categorize the problem and mitigate the impact as quickly as possible. Seeing problems and understanding the nature of the problem enables teams to make good decision to improve the situation. Without visibility, teams would be blind and unable to act.

Large-scale systems have billions of events every day and hundreds of millions of users. A monitoring solution needs to work at the same scale. As systems grow to reach new levels of scalability, there is a risk that the monitoring solution will not keep up, leaving teams blind.

End-to-End Visibility

When critical software breaks down, you want to know about it right away (see Figure 2-9). Good cloud software rarely has a catastrophic failure. There are many times when a small percentage of requests fail. At large scales, small percentages represent a large number of users. For example, a 1% failure rate across 100,000,000 users would impact 1,000,000 users! For online media, we typically target 99.9% success rate. This translates to 10 errors out of 10,000 requests. To achieve these levels, we need to see problems early. Therefore we need a smaller window to detect an error, at a rate of 1 out of 10,000 requests.

Figure 2-9. *How hot is the molten lava? A good monitoring system will tell you without needing a stick*
(Title: Dropped her car keys...Gone, man! Don't even try! Author: Colin Meusel. License: CC By 2.0)

This is very much like finding a needle in a haystack. A good monitoring system needs to capture the data and process it, looking for anomalies, fire alerts based on pre-defined rules, and provide charts and graphs to help people make sense of the data. All of these capabilities are needed to find, categorize, and fix problems.

Building a system that can do these things at scale is challenging. In many companies, building the software to figure out what just happened is a significant second effort. It is almost as if there are two software systems that need to be built: one software system to power the business and another system to measure health and vitality.

Visibility Across Services

Creating a web page for a customer requires pulling together the responses from 10-40 different service calls. Different services may be called to get the weather forecast, stock quotes, or breaking news. In addition, there are service calls to get the layout and format of the web page. In turn, these services have their own logs and connect to their own storage system. Any decent operational dashboard needs to connect these services and tie together their logs. By connecting these logs together, we could trace back user errors to failures deeper in the system.

To do this, we utilized a unique identifier for every user request. This unique identifier is called the *activity-id*. The *activity-id* is logged by every service and passed along with each service call. This *activity-id* may then be used to see all the operations associated with a user request. It sounds great, but the tools we had were slow and showed only raw logs. We wanted something faster with a visualization of data over time.

One day a senior engineer announced he had been working on something and he wanted other members of the team to see it. He had created a new instance of Elasticsearch, started putting the service logs into it, and added a Kibana dashboard on top. He had seen a lot of online conversations about an open source solution called ELK (Elasticsearch, Logstash, and Kibana) and he wanted to try it out. It took us a few days to realize that this was the perfect way to search by *activity-id* and see logs from across our system. It was a great example of letting engineers try things out. You never know what may come out from playful exploration. The ability to do rich search and create simple dashboards on application logs was invaluable.

Takeaway

Our team partnered with another team inside the company to develop a new monitoring pipeline and a set of dashboards. We would have never been able to build a large-scale monitoring pipeline without help. In addition, we built our own mini-operational datastore containing summarized measures of health across the key services. By running some simple rules on this mini-operational datastore, we got a quality of service signal for the entire platform across all datacenters. We created a web page to visualize the health of the system at a glance. There were a lot of moving pieces that all needed to work perfectly. The telemetry needed to be correct, the monitoring system needed to be up, and we needed the right rules. It all needed to work if we were to have any chance of reacting to and dealing with failures.

New Human Processes

Moving to the public cloud is wonderful because there are so many self-service tools to support development teams. The tools enable teams to deploy software updates, add hosts, and utilize storage as a service. In addition, there is a rich ecosystem of services and tools to manage the communication and tracking of daily work and emergency work. Teams now have cheap and easy ways for communicating across the organization and getting things done.

Self-service tools for managing the public cloud and consumer-oriented communication applications have matured to the point that teams may operate independently and unencumbered. Teams may now deploy code without the need to engage a separate operations team. Teams may receive direct escalations from automated scripts. In many cases, they have the power to mitigate issues without needing to bring in other functional disciplines. Teams are now directly accountable for the entire software development cycle from design through to production maintenance.

Automation

For our team, this was a change. In the past, we had been a highly matrixed organization with separate development, service engineering, and testing teams. In the past, deploying software required a large cross-functional group to package the software, verify it was ready for release, approve the deployment, and then actually perform the deployment. In the public cloud, a junior engineer could kick off the build, run the automated tests, and deploy the code. Independence changes the way teams work.

In the old system, before we moved to the public cloud, a single service engineering team would receive all alerts, they would triage the issues, and then they would escalate as appropriate. The first responders were constantly evaluating the business impact of incidents. This made sense because many operational procedures required elevated permissions and specialized tools to mitigate. As an example, a datacenter could fail. The operational response was failing away from a datacenter and changing the data replication scripts as needed. In the old system, executing a failover required administrators with elevated permissions.

We needed to rework our entire incident management flow to accommodate the new way of working. As an example, for major incidents we needed an entirely new workflow and engagement model. We also made the following important workflow changes:

- Alerts were routed directly to the correct engineering teams.

- No more tiered support model.

- Individuals working on alerts needed to determine the business impact of an incident.

- If an incident had high business impact, it was categorized as a major incident.

- Major incidents were escalated immediately, and e-mail updates were sent every hour.

These were big changes to people's roles and the way they worked together. Would our organization be able to adapt to these new ways of working together?

A Story of Security

In public cloud development, teams need to learn how to administer their systems, and they need to ensure their systems meet a wide array of quality standards. For example, development teams have a much greater role and responsibility to ensure that their systems are secure. There is a story about a development team that could not get the hardware they needed. They did have funding, and they decided to build their new project on the public cloud. This enabled the team to work around the lengthy process of purchasing hardware. The new project went forward and had a successful launch. Most of the organization was happy with the ingenuity demonstrated by the team.

The service-engineering group was the sole critical team. They were concerned that the development team lacked experience managing infrastructure, and that the public cloud enabled the team to work without proper oversight. They warned that there was a real danger of a suffering a long and impactful outage.

One day a developer ran into problems accessing the services after deploying new code to the public cloud. It was late at night so the developer decided to open up all the ports on the public cloud hosts to enable access. The developer thought it was ok, and that he would be able to fix the problem in the morning. Once the ports were open, the system worked; however, a big security hole was created in the process. Very soon after hackers found these hosts and took control of them (see Figure 2-10).

Figure 2-10. *This rusty lock should keep them out*
(Title: Bolt Security. Author: darkday. License: CC By 2.0)

With the hosts compromised, the entire project had to be shut down. After the incident, the company banned the use of public cloud services. The company needed to develop the training, processes, and technology to support proper use of public cloud services.

Takeaway

When we moved to the public cloud, administration operations were easier, safer, and could be run by any engineer. We found the ease of use also made it easy to skip over feedback and reviews from other engineering teams. To address this problem, we took feedback early from engineering teams and incorporated that feedback as standards for every service. In addition, we created new processes so that individual engineers could perform cross-functional escalations, and we provided teams with simple dashboards to assess the health of the overall system. The best management teams create processes and procedures that required constant communication, periodic evaluations of progress, and clear steps to get help. A great example is having teams come together to mitigate incidents.

Then It Gets Crazy

Rebuilding large-scale global infrastructure is risky and challenging. To reduce risk, large-scale services will typically expose new functionality to a small group of users and then expose to additional users over time. A slow rollout has a number of advantages:

- It enables validation of functionality without the need to scale to full production levels.

- It limits risk by introducing potentially breaking changes to a small audience.

- It allows targeting of new features to audience groups, like internal company users, who are more willing to provide feedback and work through technical difficulties.

- It gives the teams time to work on new tools and work together in new ways.

Table 2-2 illustrates what might be a typical technical rollout pattern used to move a large-scale system to a new software stack.

Table 2-2. *Typical Ramp-Up Plan for a Large-Scale System*

Duration	Percentage of Users	Purpose
Week 1-4	5%	Does the system work?
		Understand behavior under real-world scenarios.
		Establish baseline latency, throughput, and resource usage.
Week 5	10%	Will it scale?
		Latency should remain the same as load increases.
		Resource growth should be linear to load increases.
Week 6	20%	Are there bottlenecks or performance-related bugs?
		Look for bugs that only occur under high load.
		Look for parts of the system that are at their limits.
Week 7	30%	Are there bottlenecks or performance-related bugs?
Week 8	40%	Are there bottlenecks or performance-related bugs?
Week 9	70%	Are there bottlenecks or performance-related bugs?
Week 10	100%	Is there any traffic on the old system?
		Investigate requests going to the old system and figure out why. Come up with a plan to move all requests over to the new system.

Ten weeks may seem like a long time. Exposing a system to real user requests for the first time can yield unpredictable results. This is due to the extraordinary difficulty of artificially generating user requests for the purpose of testing.

Real user traffic has an amazing number of variations. There are variations in what is requested. There are variations in who requests the data, and variations in where the requests originate. There are variations in the timing between requests. There are even bugs in the system that may create incorrect requests. It is very, very hard to artificially create requests to match all of these variations. It is even harder to figure out which variations are naturally occurring and which variations will never be encountered. During testing, we simply do not have the time to artificially create high fidelity, real-world requests. We are time-constrained and need to do the best we can with the time allowed.

Fortunately with large-scale systems a small percentage of traffic will include almost every type of variation. In fact, 5% of user requests is often enough to be statistically significant, and this small percentage of traffic may be used to establish a model of system usage. As the real user requests grow, bottlenecks are found. Bottlenecks are parts of the system that run out of capacity and slow down the rest of the system. Often changes to configuration are enough to fix the bottleneck. As traffic increases, further bugs may appear under load. These bugs in software occur very rarely and it takes a large volume of user requests for the errors to repeat on a regular basis. Once the bug is seen and reproduced, it may be fixed. An example of a performance bug is a race condition. This occurs when two separate efforts must work together and instead they clobber each other. Race conditions typically appear after an unexpected event, like the occurrence of an error, which prevents proper coordination.

A fast ramp does not allow the team to create a model, find bottlenecks, or find performance-related bugs. In addition, a fast rollout provides little time to react when problems are found. For all of these reasons, it is good to have a gradual ramp up of real user traffic.

Let's Go Faster

For the new MSN launch we decided on a very aggressive rollout, first rolling out to corporate users at Microsoft for a few weeks, and then rolling out the new web site, new infrastructure, and new tools to all global users. With this planned global rollout, our new software would need to go from a small corporate user base to supporting a global audience with hundreds of millions of users. With very little real-world testing and no chance to work out unexpected bugs, this was going to be an incredible challenge.

There was a good reason to be aggressive. As part of the new experience, the team was busy assembling new deals with content partners. It was the structure of these deals that encouraged the aggressive rollout. There were other reasons as well. A slow rollout would have required running both systems at the same time. The editorial and content production teams would need to source, manage, and edit content in both systems. This *double publishing* was not something the organization could maintain over a long period.

After working through the details of the plan, the team decided it would be better to have a slower rollout. We decided to rollout the service to 10% of the users for one month. After that we would rollout the new services to 100% of the users in a single day. This was a better plan, but it was still very aggressive.

■ ■ ■

CHAPTER 3

A Three-Step Process for Large-Scale Cloud Services

Big, impactful efforts are full of challenges. Building new infrastructure in the public cloud brings six challenges: new technology, distributed data, integration, scale, achieving situational awareness, and new human processes. Teams need organizing principles to help them manage these risks and to successfully deliver results. Large teams, numbering in the hundreds and distributed around the globe, need clear and consistent methods to inventory, assess, and mitigate risks. Organizations have tried many different methods to manage risk, and they have experienced differing levels of success.

Learning from previous efforts is often difficult due to the informal approach taken to managing risk. In previous methods, if the explicit steps taken were not documented, it's impossible to repeat the tactics. This chapter describes a broad-based, adaptive method for managing risk. This approach worked well in other organizations, but failed to gain traction during the MSN rebuild. This chapter will look at why the approach failed, and ends with a new and different approach to managing risk.

Previous Experience

Failure was not an option (see Figure 3-1). We need to work quickly to get the teams ready for a massive launch. In 2009, I had worked at AOL and oversaw a similar effort. The team built a new version of the AOL portal from the ground up. From this successful effort I felt comfortable with developing large-scale, global applications. I planned to leverage my previous experience to implement a three-step plan. The plan was to map out the system, find all of the weaknesses and faults, and create a list of work items to make the system rugged and robust. The plan had rigor and specific steps. The plan had the advantage of being simple to teach to others, and in my mind it was proven to work. I was very wrong, and I was about to fail.

© Eric Passmore 2016
E. Passmore, *Migrating Large-Scale Services to the Cloud*,
DOI 10.1007/978-1-4842-1873-0_3

Figure 3-1. *Failure is not an option*
(Title: Failure is not an option. Author: Global X. License: CC By 2.0.)

Adaptive Approach

Working across hundreds of engineers from around the globe requires a solid plan and solid communication. In simple terms, the plan was to map out the system, find the problems, and fix them.

The plan had the following three steps:

1. Document first-level dependencies (map out the system).

2. Perform a failure mode analysis (find the weak spots).

3. Create a health model (make the system rugged and robust).

These three steps outlined a process with a heavy focus on discovery and exploration. Through these processes teams would learn and understand their system. They would discover the most important failures and gaps to address. Finally, they would identify full and partial fixes to make a rugged and robust system.

This three-step process may be adapted to almost any type of technology, industry, and size of system. A process capable of adapting so well across a broad spectrum is useful to a large audience. Any broadly applicable process requires an investment of learning to adapt those methods to the particular system, and its users.

Checklist Approach

An alternative to the three-step, adoptive process is a checklist. Checklists are the standardization of good practices specific to a particular technology, industry, and size of system. Checklist items are customized to be relevant to both the users and the system. This customization enables the checklist items to be easily understood and applied by its users. There is very little learning required to act on checklist items.

There are a number of downsides to checklists. Checklists are fixed and difficult to change. This makes checklists hard to adapt to evolving needs. Checklists prescribe tactics with the belief that following the process will result in the right outcome. Checklists do not specify the desired outcomes. This makes it impossible to separate the good and needed items in the checklist from the bad and unneeded items in the checklist. This in turn leads to lengthy and prescriptive processes for simple changes.

When choosing between different approaches, leaders need to balance the easy-to-apply, rigid checklists against the broad learning approach in the adaptive three-step process.

Bridge in the Woods

To better understand the approaches and why they failed, let's better understand the problem space. Large teams work across dozens of services. Sometimes these are small services that are called infrequently. Sometimes these are very large services that have a very large scale and are the backbone of the entire system. The design, the quality of construction, and the rigor of testing differ to match the need of each service.

Consider the analogy of building a bridge in the physical world (see Figure 3-2). There are many types of bridges. There are small wooden bridges to support people. There are large concrete and steel suspension bridges that support interstate highways. Wood is a reasonable choice of material when building small pedestrian bridges. Wood is sturdy enough for the job. In addition, wood is cheap and easy to cut to match the need. However, no one would build a mile-long, interstate highway bridge out of wood. Special steel and concrete are needed to handle the stress and load for such a big and serious concern.

Figure 3-2. *It passed the architectural review*
(Title: Shaky. Author: Nicholas A. Tonelli. License: CC By 2.0.)

Similarly, cloud services need to be evaluated by their expected usage. You need to know what type of load the service will bear. Knowing the number of requests per second at peak and the duration of requests helps you understand the workload a service may encounter. Simply put, answering these questions identifies the scope and scale of the effort. With a clear scope and scale, engineering leaders can size the effort, set the appropriate quality standards, and establish processes to ensure that those standards are met. There is no one-size-fits-all approach to building services. Organizations need processes to understand the intended usage of a system in order to build the right software structures. The three-step process acts as a guide to understanding the workload of a service and to build up quality standards and quality processes in reaction to those workloads.

First-Level Dependency

Large-scale cloud platforms are composed of many services. Services must work together to provide the desired business result. Therefore, it is not enough to understand a service in isolation. Building a rugged and robust service requires understanding how the services interact. You can think of each service relying on the other services in a staged fashion. Downstream services process commands and data in an earlier stage. Services without an intermediary service have a direct line of communication.

A first-level dependency is a downstream service with a direct line of communication.

In big systems, work is often delegated among many teams and tasks are split across many services. By breaking apart a problem into many parts, complexity is reduced, making it easier for multiple teams to work on their own part of the puzzle.

For example, there may be a content database, a web application to manage the business logic, and a directory of corporate users and privileges (see Figure 3-3). The web application depends directly on the content database. The database requires the directory of corporate users and privileges to allow access.

- The web application has a first-level dependency on the content database.

- The content database has a first-level dependency on the corporate user database.

- The web application has a second-level dependency on the corporate user database.

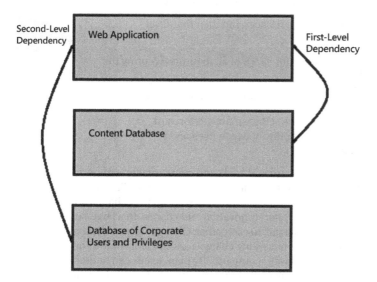

Figure 3-3. *Illustration of first-level dependencies*

Three-Step Plan

Our organization needed a method to build rugged and robust services capable of scaling to hundreds millions of users. The method we initially chose had three steps. The first step created a map of the system by documenting dependancies between services and gathering specific information to understand the workload. The second step created an inventory of possible problems and a score to find the most impactful problems. The last step used all of the information available to design improvements to manage risk and create a rugged and robust system.

Mapping out the System

Documenting dependencies is an important first step. A chain is only as strong as its weakest link. Similarly, a cloud service is only a robust as its most fragile service.

Technical leaders created a map of the entire system by collecting and documenting services along with their direct dependencies. In addition, teams were asked three questions to determine the workload of a service and to determine the flexibility of the service to change over time. These three questions documented the peak level of traffic, the expected speed of requests, and the plan for managing compatibility through changes. Answering these three questions gave the teams a solid understanding of service so they could design and build to the right quality standards. The teams needed to document the following four items for the services they owned:

1. A logical diagram of the services and their first-level dependencies

2. The expected duration for 99.9% of all requests (ignoring the slowest 0.1%)

3. The expected number of requests in a second at peak

4. A description of how the service manages forward and backward compatibility between itself and its dependencies

Documenting the plan for forward and backward compatibility is important information to collect. Software's most important quality is its flexibility and ability to change. As businesses evolve, innovation is needed to keep up with changing needs. Software needs to stay flexible to support innovation and change. In a large-scale system, there are many services that talk to each other. Changes to services may break communication between services, preventing changes and slowing innovation. By documenting the forward and backward compatibility plan, teams can understand an important aspect of flexibility and have the information needed to measure the risk of making changes.

Finding the Weak Spots

The next step is to brainstorm all the possible failures. Each team should set aside time to create a list of all the possible failures in their system. Failures include hardware failures, failures in dependencies, system slowdowns, misconfiguration of services, and failures from deployment of bad code. Thinking about failures should be a fun and fast process.

After coming up with the list of failures, the next step is to score the failures.

- What is the impact of the failure?

- How frequently will this failure occur?

Score each failure by documenting two numbers to evaluate impact and frequency. Score each failure along a 1-to-1,000 scale.

In Table 3-1, there are four categories with descriptions for impact and frequency (feel free to improve it and create your own descriptions of impact and frequency). For some organizations, it is important to categorize impact by revenue loss or by product line. Note, however, that these descriptions should apply across a large number of teams to help drive comparisons. If each team has different descriptions and different scores, the assessment will be limited in scope, and this will prevent an organization-wide view of risks.

Table 3-1. *Examples for Scoring Impact and Frequency*

Score	Impact Description	Frequency Description
1	Low impact: Less than 1% of daily active users impacted	Occurs very infrequently
10	Medium: Between 1%-10% of daily active users impacted	Occurs at least every 9 months
100	High: Partial outage in a major market	Occurs two to ten times in 12 months
1,000	Severe: Total outage in a major market or partial outage in multiple major markets	Occurs eleven or more times in 12 months

Multiply these scores together and sort all of the possible failure modes by the resulting score (see Table 3-2). Do not over-analyze the score. This is just a method to create some separation. The bigger and badder failures deserve more attention from the organization.

Table 3-2. *Examples for Failure Mode Analysis. Multiple Impact and Frequency Yield Total Score*

Description	Impact Score	Frequency Score	Total Score
Database failure	100	100	10,000
Datacenter failure	1,000	1	1,000
Web application failure	10	100	1,000
Expired certificate	100	1	100

Why a Score Matters

The score is a great tool to help leaders and managers focus on the top failure modes. It works across large organizations because it is simple, specific, and measurable. It is a simple evaluation; there are only two questions. Each question is specifically restricted to one of four answers. The numeric measurement comes as part of the selected answer. Just as important, each rung of the scale has an order of magnitude difference, yielding large numeric differences between the most and least significant failures (see Figure 3-4).

Figure 3-4. *Yeh, highest score!*

With the scores in hand, managers and leaders can look across their entire system and swarm on the most important weak spots. Swarming enables leaders to pull in experts from across the organization to work on the solutions. In addition, doing the failure mode analysis early in the process provides time for the team to come up with creative solutions to difficult situations.

Making the System Rugged and Robust

The third step is where the healing begins. It helps to establish a goal for all of the teams. Establish a not-to-exceed score for the failure modes. This will be the desired target score.

Sort the failure mode list by descending score and start at the top of the list with the item having the highest total score. For each failure mode, create a list of improvements to lessen the business impact and frequency.

Each improvement will lower the total score of the failure mode. Keep developing additional improvements until the total score is less than or equal to the desired target score.

To operationalize this process and push it out across teams, you need to be more specific and concrete. Building a health model consists of the following four steps:

- Create a set of improvements to mitigate business impact.

- Associate the mitigations to failure modes.

- Create monitors and alerts to diagnose failures and identify the proper mitigation to use.

- Automate mitigations as time and knowledge of the system allow.

For example, using Table 2-3, you could set a not-to-exceed score of 100. Start with database failure because it has the highest score, and make a plan to improve database replication by moving from a warm standby to two active databases. That will lower database failover time and lower the impact score to 10. In addition, create a new staging database to practice your database changes. The practice will drive a higher success rate and make failures less frequent. This will lower the frequency score to 10.

Progress, Not Perfection

It is important for leaders to set the right tone. Leaders should strive to use the term *mitigate business impact* when explaining the purpose of improvements. Using this wording encourages teams to explore a broader range of solutions. *Mitigate* includes partial improvements (see Figure 3-5). For example, portals like MSN, AOL, and Yahoo provide current local weather. When the weather service is not available, should these portals come to a complete standstill? No, they have decided it is better to provide a degraded solution: they serve up a page without the weather module. Exploring degraded solutions as less-bad solutions and possible improvements is the spirit of mitigation.

Figure 3-5. *An improvement over last week*
Title: Harper "backwards" Author: Heidi License: CC By SA 2.0 ©Sep 22 2012

By focusing on *business impact* teams can explore other approaches. This includes approaches that require human involvement in times of critical need. For example, if the automated process that fetches top news articles and schedules them for publication breaks, you can fall back to using the web-based tools to enter the top news stories manually. Engineering teams often think of software solutions first and try to fully automate repair actions without human intervention. Fully automated solutions require a significant engineering investment. In addition, automation of the wrong processes will simply lead to failure faster. For this reason, it is wise to explore other approaches, like human intervention. Good teams will immediately put manual processes in place and learn from those manual processes to design and build the right automated solutions. The best teams will take a crawl-walk-run approach that progressively improves the automated tools and responses.

Mitigating for business impact includes a broad range of solutions and encourages thinking of solutions outside software engineering. Good mitigations can come from product owners, editorial staff, and junior engineers. With a spirit of inclusion and openness, people of all backgrounds and experience will feel comfortable offering up improvements. It is this spirit of progress and not perfection that enables teams to feel successful and prevents them from getting stuck in analysis paralysis. Leaders will get the best out of teams when they embrace ideas from a diverse group and emphasise continuous improvement.

Continuing with the example scenario, the database needs to be monitored. You need to have awareness of any periods when requests to the database cannot be fulfilled. One possible monitoring approach is to periodically run a test against the database. This is called a *synthetic test*. The synthetic test will not cover all possible scenarios and the variance across all requests. It may miss authentication and access problems. It will certainly miss failures due to changes in database schema or stored procedures.

A better approach is to monitor the success and failure of real requests between the service and the database. In this case, you need to keep a record of requests to calculate the success rate. When the success rate drops below a threshold, the service team and the database need to be alerted.

Having a good monitoring solution in place is also needed to validate automated improvements. For example, if you improve database replication and move to two active databases, the database will automatically recover in the event of failure. You still need to validate the new setup. The team can accomplish this by running test traffic against the service and then fail one of the databases. Continuous monitoring of requests will provide evidence validating the success or failure of the new setup. A synthetic test that is run periodically may run infrequently and miss the database failure. Since synthetic tests are run infrequently, they have a small sample rate and they tend to underreport or overreport failures. This sampling problem is the downside of synthetic tests.

First Attempt at Learning (FAIL)

This three-part process did not work at all for us. Four months before launch, our teams were not ready for the big day. The teams had identified their first-level dependencies, and a few teams had completed the failure mode analysis. Not a single team had developed a health model. Watching this unfold was like watching two slow-moving cars collide. The challenges that lay ahead were clear, and we felt powerless to make a difference.

Why Documenting Dependencies Failed

Documenting dependencies did not go well. It took too long and required lots of follow-ups and reminders. There are three reasons a seemingly straightforward exercise become a drawn-out task:

- The teams were too busy with feature work and a tight timeline.

- The teams did not know how the information would be used.

- Underlying it all was a lack of trust.

Most of the work documenting dependencies was accomplished by scheduling architecture reviews for the teams. During those architecture reviews there was confusion around both the structure and the type of data that needed to be presented. Teams treated the meeting as an opportunity to walk their peers through the logical design of their services and explain why certain technologies were used. It took requests both during the meeting and after to gather first-level dependencies, latency at 99.9%, peak requests, and forward/backward compatibility plans.

Too Busy

Each of the teams was working on the mammoth effort of moving to the public cloud. The teams needed to learn an entire new set of technologies while building out new infrastructure from the ground up. With so much new work there was a certain amount of trial and error in developing new solutions. The teams were very busy creating prototypes, and then moving those prototypes into production services. The teams were constantly learning and adapting their work items to match the realities of the new technology stack. The teams were focused on getting an end-to-end service running to enable integration with other services. This left little time to write down plans and specifications.

In addition, there was a general sense that software progressed from prototype through to integration and finally onto performance and scale. Therefore, performance and throughput improvements could be made after the services were up and running. In the team's mind, performance and throughput were benchmarked after integration. These numbers were not forecasted during design. Therefore, teams felt that asking for duration at 99.9%, peak requests per second, and the compatibility plan was occurring too early in the software development lifecycle. To the teams, asking for this information during the design phases seemed like extra and unneeded homework. As a result, they put off the request for information, feeling the answers could wait until later.

Lack of Trust

The teams were not sure how the data on duration, peak request per second, dependencies, and compatibility would be used. Looking back, there was an unspoken fear that the teams would be evaluated on their responses. Teams were concerned that they would be held accountable to estimated numbers, and they did not want to set unattainable targets for performance or throughput.

Normally issues of trust can be worked through by talking. Talking through the needs of the organization, the process, and explaining how the numbers will be used has a positive impact. Dialogs around these topics will get teams involved and engaged. Trying to talk in the middle of development did not work. Teams were too busy and they were not interested in rethinking their ways of working. In the end, we communicated that data on performance and throughput could be refined and evolve over time. This message did not land. It was too brief and lacked the back-and-forth dialog needed to build trust.

Takeaway

To their credit, the teams did get the work done. They met the spirit of the request and provided the dependency analysis. Critical services provided the performance and throughput targets. We did not collect enough of the forward and backward compatibility information, and it did take too long to complete the needed work. Due to the lengthy process, we ran out of time and there was not a clear transition into the next phase, failure mode analysis.

Why Failure Mode Analysis Failed

Failure mode analysis did not go well. Very few teams completed the work. In retrospect, it is easy to see that conditions were not conducive to accomplishing the analysis.

- The work was tedious and demanded long periods of focus from busy teams.

- The teams tended to focus on very rare and impactful events.

- When pressed, the teams created an exhaustive list of data-dependent bugs.

- A central truth is that it is painful to face flaws and failures of your own making.

Failure mode analysis asks a team to find flaws in software and services they designed and constructed. Developing software is a dynamic process that employs constant problem-solving skills. Engineers take pride in solving problems and writing solid code. This sense of pride became a protective shield that cast a critical gaze beyond the software of the engineers' own making and onto the software of others.

For this reason, the failures brainstormed by the teams tended to be rare and impactful events outside their control. Often teams would first suggest events like losing power in a datacenter or a construction crew accidentally digging up a fiber cable. These were safe incidents to bring forward, as they did not shine a critical light on the team or team members. In addition, they were legitimate issues that should not be dismissed. It was a question of priority against a host of other risks and complications.

Think Horses, Not Zebras

There is an old saying from the medical and health care community:

When you hear hoofbeats, think of horses, not zebras

—Anonymous

From previous experience we know that most outages and interruptions are due to problems of our own making. A large number of business-impacting incidents and problems are the result of new code or new configurations. This has been proved out during moratoriums on changes. As evidence, consider the holiday break when there is a lockdown preventing new updates. Traditionally these lockdowns were put in place because so many people were out of the office and hard to reach.

Looking at business-impacting incidents before, during, and after the moratorium, an interesting pattern emerges. During the moratorium there is a noticeable and significant drop in incidents. Before and after the moratorium there are more incidents, with longer times to mitigate, and with more significant business impact. By any measure, lockdown periods have fewer software changes and as a result have improved stability. This shows the strong correlation between deploying new code into production and business-impacting incidents. One of the most frequent causes of business-impacting issues is the deployment of new code into production.

When brainstorming possible problems it is best to focus on the simple dangers from bugs in code, bad configuration files, or lack of capacity. These straightforward problems are the horses, and they are mostly likely the cause or trigger for business-impacting incidents. The rare and impactful events far outside the scope of ownership and control are the zebras (see Figure 3-6). They are not likely causes, and they should only be considered after the simple problems have been eliminated.

Figure 3-6. *Not the prime suspect*
(Title: Zebra. Author: Jon Mounty. License: CC By 2.0.)

When pressed to identify issues in their own systems, the teams wanted to talk about bad data from providers or poorly formatted news articles. These were real issues with a small impact to the customer experience. More importantly, this represented a single class of failures. Our teams needed to see the entire playing field. With a broad perspective they could examine multiple classes of risk and then design rugged, robust systems capable of dealing with different types of failure.

In retrospect, being self-critical is hard work. Failure mode analysis requires leaders to build a phenomenal amount of trust between themselves and their teams, and the teams need to understand how their insights will be applied. Simple stated, no team wants to give themselves a bad grade.

Takeaway

The first step to managing risk is acknowledging that risks exist. It takes a critical and dispassionate eye to spot possible failures. Leaders need more than an encouraging tone. They need to build trust and establish a culture of candor. Leaders need to invest time in talking with teams and explaining early in the software development process the reason behind brainstorming, inventorying, and scoring failures. If the organization does not invest in building a culture of candor, failure mode analysis may not achieve the desired results.

Why Developing the Health Model Failed

As an organization we ran out of time and never got to creating a health model. Creating large-scale services and running them in the cloud is relatively new. Technology has become increasingly complicated as teams take on more dependencies and build on a larger base of software and services outside their own making. Lacking the experience of developing these types of services, the new complexities and risks were difficult to see. Teams naturally focused on the problems they knew and understood.

The failure of creating the health model was a failure of leadership. It is the job of leadership to bring forward these risks in an approachable and understandable way. In addition, the leadership team needs to develop the process and structure for managing risks and set high standards to ensure quality. What worked with one organization may not work in a different organization.

As an organization, we were in denial. Software and services were working at a smaller scale. In the face of working software, the emerging risks were easy to ignore (see Figure 3-7). We had not spent enough time analyzing our software to ensure it would be healthy under the load and stresses of a global user base. Lacking this key analysis, our organization assumed the underlying platform was stable with few failures.

Figure 3-7. *We have the perfect health plan
(Title: IMG_7887. Author: Jane Hayes. License: CC By 2.0.)*

DevOps KungFu Masters

With four months to go, most of the feature work was nearing completion. The systems had been designed, built, and were in the process of being tested. Making changes at this late stage was not very desirable. Yet we needed to make a lot of changes. We needed to add in new features and functionality to make our services and our software rugged and able to withstand failures.

The previous three-step method was a flop. We needed to do something quickly to get ready for the big launch. The three-step process consisted of the following:

1. Document first-level dependencies.

2. Complete failure mode analysis.

3. Create a health model.

Completing these steps took time; it required learning new concepts and coming up with disciplined analysis. Our busy and stretched teams were already learning a new technology by moving to the cloud. They needed less learning, and they desired more practical, immediately applicable advice.

To get our teams into shape, we needed to start over from the beginning. We needed to create DevOps KungFu masters. We needed to teach through imitation and repetition (see Figure 3-8). Over time, concepts could be added to the practice. We decided to get specific, be explicit, and let teams react to a checklist of tasks. We created a checklist with all of the work that needed to get done. This checklist would contain an explicit set of tasks for each team to ensure their services were fault tolerant.

Figure 3-8. Just Do It. Less classroom, more hands-on study

A small group of five assembled to create the checklist. We did not know of anyone else who had done something similar. We did not know if this would work. We were running out of options and we needed to try something.

CHAPTER 4

Success

In reaction to the failure of the three-step approach, we decided to take a new approach and build a checklist of must-do items. In this chapter, I describe the checklist, the management tactics used to change direction, and the reaction of the teams to the checklist. We had to learn by doing and in this chapter I share our experience of making a big change.

The Rollout

We needed to be specific, and we needed to assemble a detailed list of tasks. For a few hours, five of us got in a room. We created a checklist with 76 items. Our checklist had four major categories:

- A Pre-release section with 13 items (out of 76)

- A Monitoring section with 29 items (out of 76)

- A Deployment section with 11 items (out of 76)

- A Mitigation section with 23 items (out of 76)

With the checklist in hand, the questions were how to start, and how to drive the implementation across a big, global distributed set of teams. No one had experience pushing out a detailed checklist. There was simply no model to work off of to deploy this new effort, engage the teams, and get the needed work done. We would need to learn by doing. We needed to become a fit organization capable of daily deployments while maintaining high uptimes through constant readiness. With little time before a critical launch we needed hands-on experience. We decided to introduce the checklist in three successive waves.

- We started by asking teams to complete seven checklist items.

- Then we asked the teams to complete 65 of the remaining 69 checklist items.

- We finished by turning on the alerts, sending them directly to the development teams.

© Eric Passmore 2016

E. Passmore, *Migrating Large-Scale Services to the Cloud*,
DOI 10.1007/978-1-4842-1873-0_4

The checklist and the first seven items were a shift in direction from the previous method. It would take weeks to thoroughly explain the reason for the change in direction to hundreds of engineers seated in three different continents. That was time we did not have. Instead, we explained the reason for the shift and the expectations of the seven items to a handful of top-level managers.

To formalize the seven items, we had a project manager enter the seven tasks into each team's work item queue. The beta release would be the first time we went public with a portion of our user base. Working back from the launch date, we set the due dates for the seven items to a month before the beta release. We followed up by asking for weekly status and progress updates.

This fast, top-down rollout made some teams uncomfortable. This was new, high-priority work that appeared out of thin air. In addition, teams needed to ramp up and learn the tools needed to complete the tasks. Happily, instead of pushing back on the work, the teams took the time to read the seven tasks. There was little push back for four reasons. Most importantly all teams were doing this work, no one was singled out. A team that pushed back would single themselves out as special or different, a distinction teams did not want. In addition, the timing was right as the teams finished their feature work and started to think more about production. Each task seemed like a good and needed step to take as part of our launch preparations. There were only seven specific work items, and it was easier to do the work and not push back. The teams dug in and started worked on the seven tasks. Progress was uneven, with work occurring in bursts and at different rates across teams. However, in the end, the seven tasks were completed on time.

After the first seven tasks were completed, we assigned the other 69 items. We asked the teams to choose what to work on, and we asked them to complete 95%, or 65 assigned items. Again, we entered the work items into each team's work item queue. Entering these work items was a long and tedious process. It took one person two days to enter the remaining checklist items.

Moving to the second stage was another fast rollout without enough time to properly communicate the context and background for why these items were assigned to teams. Again, we worked with the same group of top-level managers to explain the need for more work items. There was surprisingly little push-back from the teams on the additional work items because the checklist items were reasonable, appropriate, and sobering. They showed all of the hidden work needed to make services reliable. Teams who saw the checklist items felt these were good and necessary things to do. Therefore, much of the support came from the credible and sensible nature of the checklist items. Teams had a hard time arguing against doing the right thing.

A month before the full public release the alerts were turned on. These alerts went directly to the developers' mobile phones. This was a chance to practice managing alerts, communicate across teams, and refine implementation before going live. During the previous months, the date for going live with alerts had been communicated multiple times across both senior leaders and development teams. In addition, training sessions and brownbags were held to make sure the teams knew how to use the tools and how to ask for help. This preparation, for monitoring, alerting, and mitigating processes, paid off and there was support from all levels of the organization to turn on the alerts a month before going live to all customers.

Failure Injection

In the first chapter, I mentioned the risks involved in moving large-scale systems into the cloud. Walking through a detailed list of risks is useful information, but it does not yield specific actions. The simplest way to move from theory to practice is to purposely break things.

During software development, teams typically develop services assuming all is well and working properly. The real world is different. It is filled with risks and failures. It is said that no plan survives contact with the enemy, and similarly no new cloud service will run problem-free. What if teams could see the impact of failures before reaching production?

Breaking things on purpose is called *failure injection*, and it is a great way to develop concrete and specific work items to make systems more rugged and robust. Examples include purposely stopping services, taking databases offline, and reducing capacity to the point of failure. Causing these problems will expose weaknesses that need to be addressed.

It is best to schedule failure injection tests before going to production. Early failure testing in a safe environment has the obvious benefit of eliminating customer impact. In addition, doing failure injection tests early provides early feedback to teams and enables them to come up with better designs. For all of these reasons, you should incorporate failure injection testing into the development lifecycle of your services.

Seven Rules

The seven tasks covered monitoring, alerting, and most importantly validating successful completion of the work. We manually failed services and checked to ensure alerting and logging was done correctly. The service failures were scheduled by the central Service Engineering team while the development teams assessed their own success.

1. Each team created one alert on their own service using raw counters.

2. Each team created one alert on a dependant service using synthetic probes.

3. Each team failed their application and validated their alerts.

4. We failed the central storage system and each team validated their alerts.

5. Each team ensured that errors were logged.

6. We logged all requests into a central monitoring service.

7. Each team completed on-call duty training.

Alerts Using Raw Counters

These seven items were selected because they had the highest impact in reducing risk. At the very top of the list was a work item to create an alert using raw counters. Creating an alert would measure the vitality of the service and show if the system was healthy or sick. This one measure created a critical feedback loop as the service changed. As code and configuration changed we could evaluate the impact to service health.

Synthetic Testing on a Dependent Service

The second item asked teams to monitor the health of their critical downstream services. Having an awareness of these dependencies was needed to diagnose integration issues in a complex system with many moving parts. In a complex system with many services and many teams there is a tendency to work in two modes: either deep investigation of your own team's services or blaming other teams's dependant services. Alerts on downstream services provided a quantifiable measure to direct the investigation and prevent finger pointing. We had a choice to create these alerts from raw counters or from synthetic probes. Getting raw counters, event logs, and the context on when to alert from other teams was not easy. We decided to use synthetic probes because they were easy to create and easy understand due to their pass or fail nature.

Failure Injection to Validate Alerts

The third work item was validation of the first item, self-monitored health from raw counters. The teams were expected to fail their service, show the service health decline, and raise an alert. This simple test was easy to run and it ensured that the service would fire an alert when an outage occurred. It would make sure alerts had the right information and that the alerts were directed to the correct team.

Failure Injection on Central Storage

The fourth work item validated all alerts, both self-monitored health and dependency checks. Almost every service depended on the central storage system. By failing that central system no reads or writes could get through. This failure was a massive disruption, and it tested the alerting coverage for all teams. This large, coarse-grained failure ensured that teams would be aware when components deep inside the platform failed. It would also make sure alerts were sent to the correct teams.

Logging Errors

The fifth work item covered an important step often missed on the journey from development to production. Error logs are often misconfigured. Typically two problems occur. Very frequently the production error logs continue to capture debug information. When the service takes live traffic, the logs are filled with too much background data, making real errors hard to find. In the worse cases, the large volume of debug logs fills up the disk and causes the service to fail. In the second case, error logs are turned off or configured to a non-existent location. This fifth item was needed to make sure the error logs were captured and that they were meaningful.

Logging to a Central Location

The sixth item was intended to capture the forensic information needed for later investigations. When problems did occur, we needed information to assess the business impact and find the cause of the issue. Too often these logs are turned off or stored for a very short period of time. By managing the logs centrally, any team could search through all the logs and gather the needed information. The primary purpose of this request was to ensure transparency through accessible historical records. The secondary purpose was to validate that teams were retaining their application and request logs.

Completing On-Call Training

The seventh item was a recognization that we needed to work together in new ways. When a business-impacting incident did happen, we wanted to be prepared. The training to manage incidents was essential if we were to communicate and operate effectively in times of crisis.

Takeaway

These first seven items yielded great results. Teams rallied to the real-world scenario of failing services. No one wanted to seem unprepared during the scheduled tests. Teams learned how to use the synthetic testing service, then learned how to configure alerts, and then started to learn the incident management tools. More importantly, the basic alerts were validated by working through the seven work times. After running the failure injection tests, some teams found their alerts misconfigured. As a result, the alerts did not reach the team. Configuration issues were easily fixed, and the teams were eager to close the obvious gaps.

There were some interesting discoveries. During the scheduled failure of the central storage system some services unexpectedly remained healthy. We discovered that these healthy services used their own storage accounts, and they did not use the central system. Using separate accounts was not a problem as long as the service was rugged and robust and ready to handle failures. More importantly, the organization had a better understanding of the dependancies between systems and the patterns of failure we were likely to see in production.

These seven items were chosen because they provided situational awareness and created a feedback loop to drive learning. They created a link of causality between the changes we made and any negative impact to the system. Linking changes to outcomes would enable teams to operate independently and amplify the changes that worked while minimizing the changes that failed.

A Tale of Two Earthquakes

If your organization is serious about building large-scale services, make an effort to set high standards for ruggedness and robustness and do not shy away from asking teams to adopt the same set of technology. A 2010 *Time Magazine* article by Tim Padgett called "Chile and Haiti: A Tale of Two Earthquakes" examined the different fates of two regions devastated by earthquakes. In 2010, just weeks apart, two earthquakes struck Haiti and Chile. In Haiti, the earthquake killed 200,000 people. In Chile, the earthquake was 500 times stronger and killed hundreds of people. It is shocking that a more powerful earthquake would result in exponentially fewer deaths. Chile's building codes are credited for enforcing the use of better materials and construction methods. It is these building codes that made the difference and gave Chile a better outcome.

Similarly, there should be standards for large-scale systems in the cloud. Companies like Facebook, Google, Amazon, and Microsoft are increasingly mandating the use of common services. These services are designed to run across multiple datacenters and be rugged, robust, and scalable. By using these services, teams do not need to build their own infrastructure, and leaders can focus teams on building features to delight their customers.

Does your organization have standards for building cloud infrastructure? Who gets to select the technology and how is that technology evaluated? More importantly, how is that technology rolled out and put into production? These are tough questions to address due to the rapid advancement and changes in technology. Technology continues to change and improve, making it hard to create lasting standards.

The key is to focus on generic services and solutions that solve a common need. Storage services that can manage documents and blobs of JSON or XML may be adapted across many different types of applications. These storage solutions should be rugged, robust, and able to withstand failure. When teams use these standard solutions, their services become stronger and better able to handle failure.

Importance of Deployment

The capability of deploying software does not get enough love. Teams with a box software background or an application background are completely removed from the deployment process. Box software is shipped to customers who independently install it on their own devices. Applications are deployed via the online store. As a result, many teams lack an appreciation of how hard it is to reliably deploy software at scale.

The checklist covered deployment as a specific sub-category. It is important to have explicit work items around deployment. Large-scale cloud services need to deploy software updates to thousands of hosts in multiple datacenters. Software needs to be deployed quickly; no one wants to wait for hours watching deployments. Software deployment needs to be reliable; it is impossible to manually retry when there are thousands of hosts. Software deployment needs to be non-invasive; it cannot cause outages or downtime.

Teams that are new to online services often lack an understanding of the important role that good deployment plays in getting updates out into production. The checklist helped to educate teams and show them the whole playing field with regard to deployments. The checklist listed out the important features needed for a good deployment system.

An example is the checklist item for fast rollback (item 28). Teams need to be able to roll back to the last know good state in minutes. Accomplishing this at scale requires additional infrastructure. It is a recommended practice to store both the previous version and the next version of the software on the host. By having multiple versions already on the host, rolling back is simplified and made faster. No new packages need to be assembled or deployed; rolling back merely requires pointing to the old build and doing a restart.

Response to the 69 Work Items

The reaction to the additional 69 checklist items was positive. Teams felt the checklist items were clear and readable, and were general improvements. When teams did not understand the intent or purpose of a set of checklist items, they asked questions. In summary, by providing an explicit list, teams could explore the items at their own pace and react to the checklist items. The checklist items were simple and did not require new investigations to learn.

When rolling out a checklist of items, it is important to stress that all teams are doing the work. Many teams will push back if they feel they are working alone. The knowledge that everyone is going in the same direction is comforting.

Implementing the checklist was not trouble-free. In conversations with the teams, we discovered that all error and request logs were going to a single namespace in the test account. Pouring all of the logs into one location was a huge problem; it was impossible to separate the meaningful errors and requests from the background requests. The test account was a problem only in that it had a reduced service level agreement and experienced longer downtimes.

It is easy to see how teams ended up with a single location for all logs. The teams were busy and they copied the messaging and logging code from each other. The production logging service required an encryption key, but the test account was encryption free. Once the service went into production, this setup would not be able to scale; the logging service would get overloaded with requests, and queries on an overburdened system would not be possible.

We needed more checklist items to highlight the right structure for these logs and error messages. The Quality of Service team interviewed the teams and found the team with the best structure and setup for logs and errors. They documented these standards and held sessions to explain the improvements. The plan was to have each team implement these new standards and improvements, and a project manager was assigned to track the progress of these checklist items.

Scaling DevOps Practices

When taking new practices and scaling them across large orgs, leaders will encounter teams who see the tasks as outcomes to achieve. They are not interested in the learning that accompanies the work. We found that it is a good idea to separate doing the work from mastering the skills. Establish separate training sessions to gain mastery or build self-service tools to enable teams to ramp up quickly.

While rolling out the improvements to the logging of errors, something strange happened. The teams did not embrace the new work items. Instead, the senior engineers got together and requested the work be done in a different way. They felt the logging work was common work that should be done by a centralized team.

Having a common team do the work was not the best approach. To effectively query the logs, each team needed to understand how the logs were managed and stored. If the teams did their own work to set up the logs, they would be ready in emergencies to query the logs and gather diagnostic information. Although the work should not be centralized, there existed a great deal of centralized infrastructure with a common logging client, common formats, and common tools. The engineers insisted that a central team was the best approach to address the checklist items. They decided to organize a virtual team and centralize the work. In the end, a single, central, virtual team did all of the log setup. As a result, the individual teams lacked the experience with the logging service and so the teams struggled to query the logs. During production incidents, we lost time because teams needed to first learn the basics of the logging system.

The Importance of Drilling

We standardized much of the backend infrastructure. Storage, image processing, video processing, and queries were all replicated across four datacenters. These services had enough redundancy and capacity to handle the failure of an entire datacenter. Validating the design and getting everything to work was a huge challenge.

It took six attempts before we got the datacenter failover right.

The system was backed by a solid architecture, and each step in the failover process was carefully crafted by the team. Two months before the beta launch we had plenty of data in the system. New video and images were processed every day. It seemed like the right time to fail a datacenter and watch the system recover. The failover test consistence of the following four steps:

1. Stop writes to the primary, master datacenter.

2. Run a process to flush out writes to the slave datacenter.

3. Make the slave datacenter the new primary, master datacenter.

4. Examine all of the services to ensure they have moved over correctly.

We assembled a team of software developers, their managers, and the Quality of Service team. We initiated the datacenter failure and it did not work. There were too many moving pieces and the orchestration of moving all the upstream services did not go as planned. From that first attempt we learned a lot and made adjustments to improve the failover.

Every time we tried to complete a failover, little details would trip us up. It took six attempts before we finally got all the steps perfect and ready for production. In retrospect, these drills were critical for the team. During an emergency, you rise to your level of training. These six failover attempts provided the training and the confidence for the team to perform the failover.

These were public attempts communicated across all teams. As the other teams saw the effort and eventual success, they developed a sense of confidence in the underlying infrastructure. Drilling and using the experience of those drills to make improvements is very important. A month before the planned public beta we ran another failure injection test of a key central service. This time something very different happened.

All of the teams had followed the checklist and created synthetic tests on the central services. When the central service went down, all the alerts went off. This time the alerts were all assigned to the central service team! The central team ended up with a new alert every five minutes from every team. There were hundreds of duplicated alerts assigned to one team.

We used this experience to establish an improved practice: each team was responsible for its own health monitoring, and teams should only assign alerts to themselves. Teams continued to track the health of their direct dependancies and used this information for diagnostic purposes. To keep the alerts at a reasonable level, alerts for dependant services were assigned a low severity. Having a low severity allowed the alerts to be filtered out and prevented teams from getting a page or midnight call when a service outside their ownership experienced a service interruption. Teams used monitoring on raw counters to evaluate the health of their own services and created high-severity alerts only for their own services.

Teams were asked to provide their dependant services with their tests. The central teams could take these tests and run them to verify everything was working correctly before a new release. Having the teams share automated tests created a common sense of *healthy*. Sharing these tests created a more transparent environment and helped build trust between teams.

Beta Launch

Public beta would introduce our large-scale cloud service to 10% of real users for one month. Our services had hundreds of millions of users. The beta test was estimated to bring in ten million users. This was a true test. There were real consequences to customers during product incidents. During the beta launch, the site stayed up and available to customers. The beta period was our transition from software development into managing a large-scale cloud service.

Our checklist drove monitoring and alerting across the teams. The checklist was too successful! High-severity alerts fired at the smallest sign of trouble. A small slowdown might generate hundreds of alerts. We never expected so many alerts and so many problem tickets. For example, a back-end ingestion process failed, only to succeed with an automated retry 30 seconds later. These types of issues had little to no business impact.

Teams raced around looking into every problem with commendable diligence. Each high-severity alert generated a phone call to the on-duty team members, and they were overwhelmed with noisy events. Over time the teams improved and started to lower severity on non-critical alerts. They began to filter out the noise. During the beta period, we learned how to separate the noisy events from the true impactful events.

The teams learned how to use the tools during the beta period. Through continuously exercising the incident management tools, querying the logs, and checking diagnostics, they became proficient at gathering data and taking corrective action.

In the pressure of the beta launch, the teams made an effort to work together for the greater good.

The teams learned how to work together and embraced the new workflows. Everyone knew this was a big moment, and they put aside their own local concerns to drive business value. The teams shared their tips and techniques for working around problems. Every day teams would request help and hand off incidents to other teams.

Production Launch

When we finally did launch at full scale, we were ready. With the huge surge of user traffic, the site stayed up. We had the capacity, the scale, and the safety measures to serve our customers. It was a proud moment for all of the teams as we moved from a ten-year-old platform to a modern set of cloud services.

The hard work by the teams paid off. They deserve credit for the success. The checklist helped focus the work and gave the teams the right perspective as they made tradeoff decisions between features and operational stability.

CHAPTER 5

▪ ▪ ▪

What We Learned

Looking back, there is one big takeaway: blow things up. Failure injection testing was the single most valuable exercise because it generated real-world outcomes. The explicit checklist established standards and expected outcomes. Failure injection shined a light on the gaps between real-world outcomes and the expected outcomes documented in the checklist. Teams were surprised by these gaps. These surprises drove the teams to investigate. Therefore, doing coarse-grain failure injections drives learning.

- **Everyone learns**: Failing big services causes faults across all of the teams and services.

- **Create surprise**: Use failures to validate the checklist of monitoring, alerting, and mitigations.

- **Work together**: Large failures drill and prepare teams to work across functional areas and solve problems.

Break things on purpose. Teams learn when they are surprised by the results and they investigate.

As an example, take checklist item 25 (deployments should not degrade availability of the service). To complete this item, engineering teams designed a deployment process with the goal of maintaining high availability. As part of development, the team created a metric to measure availability before, during, and after a deployment. During testing, the team looked to see if deployments impacted service availability. When a deployment reduced availability, the team investigated, found the cause, improved the deployment process, and learned along the way.

Very rarely do things work as expected the first time around. It takes many rounds of improvements and trials to get complicated technology working smoothly. These multiple iterations give the team time to drill and prepare for the real event. Drilling on a failure several times improves the communication between teams, and the practical experience provides data to help drive confident decision-making.

© Eric Passmore 2016
E. Passmore, *Migrating Large-Scale Services to the Cloud*,
DOI 10.1007/978-1-4842-1873-0_5

Coarse-grained failure injection testing is the single best thing to build strong teams capable of responding well during incidents. Creating failures forces teams to drill and practice. For example, if fault injection as part of deployments was done the teams would drill and be better prepared for similar real world scenarios. Take for example if a deployment is taking a long time. The teams would have only practiced broken deployments, and therefore had no previous experience with slow deployments. Still teams will know where to look for status information. The teams will be familiar with using the tools, they will know what steps to take, and who should execute those steps. In addition, they will be comfortable communicating the current business impact, the path to mitigate, and the expected time to complete the mitigation.

Risk Managing New Technology

We were able to manage the risks of new technology through benchmarking and prototyping with clear, measurable goals. These goals were the duration of requests at the 99.9% level and the requests per second at peak. These clear goals pushed teams to benchmark performance and try out different configurations. The data from benchmarking informed the architecture and enabled the teams to evolve the architecture to make the best use of the technology.

Benchmark new technology and use an evidence-based approach to inform the architecture.

Risks from Distributed Data

We were able to manage the risk of multiple datacenters by standardizing on a few central services and thoroughly testing them. We created a single storage service that managed state and handled replication between datacenters. This is a big-bet strategy, and it may seem counterintuitive to rely on a single central service.

Big bets are needed. Creating a geo-diverse solution is complicated and requires input from experts in different functional areas. The best approach is to invest the best experts to create centralized capabilities used by all teams. To get the right solution, we invested the experts on our team, and brought in experts from Azure. With the help of these experts we made use of the latest features, and we were able to create a special physical allocation of storage to reduce hotspots and maximize throughput.

A big-bet approach created a focused effort. That focus enabled more testing time and deeper testing. We had the resources to invest in failure testing, and early on we tested the ability to recover from failure. This testing revealed a problem in our design that we identified and corrected.

Recognize geo-redundant, multiple datacenters services as a big bet and invest your experts in a few centralized storage and replication capabilities.

Risks from Integration

We were explicit about backward and forward compatibility, and we created long-lasting APIs that did not change. We developed and deployed the APIs into production before the functionality was available. This was possible because we documented what requests would work, and used mock objects to fake the responses. Teams were able to see and code against the APIs four weeks after the project started.

It is never too early to integrate. Leaders need to make sure integration between services happens during development. Integration enables discovery of issues. Therefore early discovery provides time to investigate and develop the right solution. Late integration leads to late discovery. Late discovery in turn leads to workarounds that shim APIs to match unexpected patterns. These workarounds create unmanageable and difficult to use APIs that will slow down all future work by requiring new developers to learn the quirky patterns and extensive testing to validate functionality.

As an example, our system required logos for each article. The logos were stored separately from the articles. The front-end team pulled all of the logos when the application started and put the data into a long-lived cache. This workaround pulled huge amounts of data at application startup. During deployments, all applications would be restarted and these big requests saturated the network and slowed down all requests. Later we developed an improved API that returned the article along with the required logo. Had we found this issue early we could have developed a better solution and prevented the performance drag during deployments.

Leaders need to drive work items early in the development to ensure stable APIs along with forward and backward compatibility between consumers and producers.

Risks from Working at a Big Scale

We were able to see all of the interactions between systems only after blowing things up. By mapping out the first-level dependencies we developed an understanding of the relationships between services. Failure injection testing revealed surprising gaps in our understanding. During failure injection tests, services that should have failed stayed up. These services stayed up because they did not rely on the central storage solution. They relied on a different technology for storage. This was unexpected, and we were glad to correct our understanding.

This better understanding enabled us to create real-world recovery and mitigation plans. We drilled by performing coarse-grained failure tests multiple times until we got it right. During those drills, we amplified the things that worked and diminished the things that did not work.

When dealing with complexity, practice trumps theory.

Risks From Lack of Situational Awareness

We established a checklist of standard monitoring and alerting practices to ensure we had the data necessary to triage, diagnose, and investigate problems. We needed a solution that would scale to meet our needs, and we partnered with a central team to develop the right solution.

Building your own monitoring solution is rarely a competitive advantage; consider partnering with others or purchasing solutions to meet your monitoring and alerting needs.

Risks from New Human Processes

Our teams came together during the beta period. With real users the teams felt a sense of responsibility, so they put aside their own perspectives to work to the greater good. This spirit of taking things as they come enabled the teams to adapt to new ways of working and to suggest improvements.

Gradually ramp up usage of your new system. This slow start will give teams time to work together and adapt to new ways of working.

Proving Mastery Through Failure Injection

Have you ever taken something apart and failed to put it back together? True experts have no problem demonstrating mastery by reassembling complex systems. With large-scale cloud services there are no physical parts and pieces to manage. How do organizations demonstrate mastery? We found that taking the simple standard of being available to the consumers in the face of large failures was an accurate proof of mastery. If we injected a big failure and the teams were able to recover in a reasonable amount of time, it was proof that we knew what we were doing. In summary, recovery from large failures demonstrates mastery of complex software systems.

Recovery from large failures demonstrates mastery of complex software systems.

Checklist Takeaways

Some parts of the checklist worked really well and they saved the day. In other ways the checklist missed the mark and did not cover critical areas. Below is a summary of our experience with the checklist. Each of the four checklist sections is covered: Pre-Release, Deployment, Monitoring, and Mitigation. For each section, a summary of what worked is provided along with areas for improvement.

Pre-Release: What Worked Best

The checklist focused our organization on creating a central approach to tooling and support. We used the same tools for all systems all around the world. We had the same incident management solution, the same monitoring solution, the same alerting solution, and the same log management solution. Using the same tools is not always a good idea. A tool can force a workflow that does not make sense for all teams. Tools may not integrate with the right datasources, forcing teams to migrate. A common approach worked in our case because the tools were good. They had advanced features that automated a great deal of work, and the workflow could be tweaked to match each team. As part of the move to Azure all of the teams had centralized the logs and data into central repositories.

There were three advantages to having the same set of tools. First, engineers shared knowledge and tips between teams. Using the same tools and the same workflow drove a lot of commonality, and pretty soon everyone was speaking the same language. Teams started to share the techniques they used to suppress noisy alerts and the ways they improved diagnostics. In addition, teams built their own extensions to tools and they were able to share their work. The second advantage was the visibility from having a single solution. Anyone with permission could mine logs across teams. The cross-team view was fantastic when we were looking for bottlenecks or needed more data to show a system-wide issue. Third, teams built trust in the tools. Everyone was invested in a single set of tools. This commitment made a difference as teams adapted to the new tool workflows. When teams ran into issues, they made constructive suggestions.

We built our own capacity reporting tools, and they filled an important need. Self-provisioning tools in the public cloud make it very easy to add or reduce capacity. We created a weekly report to monitor the capacity used by each team and forecasted spending for the budget period. As new features get added, performance and throughput could degrade. Degraded throughput meant the services would need additional capacity. The weekly report showed us these changes in capacity and enabled us to prioritize improvements to throughput. The reporting system enabled teams to make local decisions while allowing the organization to optimize spending. The alternative would have been an approval process to add capacity. That approval process would have defeated the whole point of self-provisioning tools.

Pre-Release: Areas for Improvement

As we began daily deployments we found we did not have enough automated testing. As a result, there were gaps in our end-to-end scenario coverage. We needed extensive manual tests and verification. Manual testing was expensive, and we did it in one pass at the end of the day. Bugs and issues could have been found sooner. The early discovery of issues would have created a faster and more powerful feedback loop. As a result, about half of our release candidates failed to make it into production, and teams needed to set aside a significant amount of time to fix issues and improve testing.

Deployment: What Worked Best

Deployment is an important capability in a large-scale cloud service. Doing deployments at scale in the public cloud is a significant capability that needs to work. There are thousands of hosts across multiple datacenters that all need to get the same software. The deployment process needs to be smart enough to automatically skip bad hosts or risk delaying the entire deployment due to one bad host. Public cloud services are free to take down hosts and bring up new hosts. In this case, the deployment needs to automatically kick in for the new hosts and do a full install. Sometimes old hosts are brought back online with old versions of software. The deployment process needs to detect these old versions and catch the host up with the latest version of the software.

Thanks to the checklist we were confident in our deployment process. We worked hard to build in three key features to support a robust and rugged system. Most importantly, we always had two versions of the application on each host. We always loaded in v-previous and v-next versions. Switching between each version was automated and could be trigged with a configuration change. Having both versions enabled us to quickly roll back in the event of an incident. We never needed to search for a working version of the application; it was always ready to go at a moment's notice.

The checklist clearly established a principal of deployment without degradation of the customer experience. We wanted to keep our services available and running well even during a deployment. We did not meet this goal when we first started doing deployments. Having established a standard created a feedback loop that enabled rapid improvement.

Another checklist item was evaluating a new software release on a small number of hosts before pushing the update to all hosts. We did this by pushing the update to a small number of production hosts, and then we ran a few basic tests. The tests ran in our production environment before we enabled live traffic. These tests found issues before we rolled out the release. Evaluating in production before going big with a change is a recommended practice for all services and all teams.

Deployment: Areas for Improvement

When we launched, we lacked good diagnostics on deployments. When a deployment ran into trouble, we did not always know there was a problem and we had a hard time diagnosing problems. We needed help, and we often brought in an external support team.

Deployment is an important capability necessary to support the business. Rapid deployment enables rapid responses and minimizes business impact during outages. Rapid deployment also enables new features and new experiments to drive greater business value. A deployment system that works well and quickly, enables the business to try out new ideas. A bad deployment system will create friction by delaying experiments, and may possibly force the business to ration their new ideas. When good features are discovered, a bad deployment system will take time and slow the exposure of those ideas to a broader audience.

During the launch of the new MSN there were times when we needed to deploy straight into production with very little testing. An obvious example was during business-impacting outages when the site slowed down or ran short of capacity. In those cases, we would run in a degraded capacity and turn off the most resource-expensive services. We needed to deploy configuration files to make these changes. In other cases, we had very good site enhancements that were implemented in a low-risk way. We had the ability to expose new features to a small portion of the audience. We also had the ability to kill experiments and move all users to the known good version of the software. We might deploy several times a day, pushing out new experiments and tweaks to the site. We wanted to rapidly adjust and improve our site day over day.

Unfortunately, our deployment system often ran into slowdowns and other problems. In the beginning, this prevented our teams from deploying several times a day. In retrospect, we should have had better diagnostics to help us pinpoint issues in deployments.

Monitoring: What Worked Best

Two months before launch we started treating alerts as production incidents. If needed, on-call engineers would get up in the middle of the night to fix issues. With each passing week the team's cohesiveness and decision quality made dramatic improvements. We raced ourselves into shape. It was hard at first, but it paid off in the end.

Monitoring: Areas for Improvement

We had lots of false alarms and noise from our monitoring. Many of our monitors were synthetic probes. Synthetic probes run at intervals, sampling the response from a server. Teams would establish rules to raise alerts. For example, a team might create a rule to raise an alert only after three out of five web pages failed or timed out. Due to the small sample size, the synthetic probes tended to underreport or overreport problems. The synthetic probes only had the request and response; they did not have internal diagnostics. As a result, synthetic probes over reported issues resulting in false alarms. Over time teams ignored the alerts from synthetic probes.

Mitigation: What Worked Best

There were two practices that really helped improve our response to production incidents. The first was discussed at the beginning of the chapter: coarse-grained failure injection. Failure injection tests exposed gaps in our monitoring and alerting. In addition, the drills from failure injection tests were practice runs that created a well-defined process for mitigation.

Propagation of *active-ids* through the logs was another practice that dramatically improved our diagnostics. As discussed in Chapter 2, *active-ids* enabled cross-stack investigation. It was easy to find reproducible cases and hand off example requests to downstream teams. For example, if a web page timed out because the storage service was slow, the *active-id* would tie together all of the requests. The investigating team could find all of the underlying requests called to serve the web page and see the very slow response from storage. The investigating team would then send the storage team the logs along with the HTTP requests for the storage service.

Mitigation: Areas for Improvement

Shifting from developing a large-scale service requires a significant change in thinking. Instead of following the scripted mitigation steps, engineering teams had a tendency to look for the root cause. We had a goal of mitigating the business impact from high-severity alerts in 90 minutes and fully repairing the problem within a week. Teams really wanted to find out what was wrong and why the system was not functioning as expected. Full investigations took a long time and as a result we would miss our 90-minute goal for mitigations.

As an example, a new web application had a race condition that caused the service to hold onto resources and not release them. After running for two hours, the web application got low on resources and started to slow down. Finding and fixing the race condition would be a lengthy process, but rolling back the web application would be a quick and effective mitigation. Once mitigated, the team could spend time investigating and fixing the code bug that caused the problem.

Sharing and Modifying the Checklist

One of the surprising things about the checklist is how many times it has been requested. Other teams have expanded the checklist by adding new items. One team even took the checklist and created a progression of four levels. Each level added new items to increase ruggedness and maintain uptime in the event of failure. It is great to see the checklist grow and be adapted to new situations.

CHAPTER 6

Pre-Release and Deployment Checklist

Just ship, baby.

—Kent Beck

Large-scale cloud services for a global audience need to meet user demand by scaling; they need to be world-ready with market customizations; they need to be secure; they need to manage privacy considerations; and they need to integrate with partners. That is a lot to remember, so we decided write down the work items behind these requirements. These work items are requirements for a large-scale global application, and they became the Pre-Release Checklist.

There are two types of requirements: explicit and implicit. The explicit asks are provided to the engineering teams. The implicit requirements are expected, and rarely communicated, to the engineering teams. Typically, requirements for performance, privacy, security, and market customizations are not explicitly provided. It takes people with prior experience to identify these needs and to explain how to accomplish these goals. The very heart and soul of the checklist is to make implicit tasks explicit. Some of the checklist items are outcomes and are referred to as the *whats*. Other checklist items are procedural points and are referred to as the *hows*. The following are examples of each from the Pre-Release Checklist:

- **How**: Versions for all assets in production

- **What**: Prevent URL manipulation

Pre-Release Checklist

The Pre-Release Checklist items should be implemented during the software development process. Waiting to implement these items after development would require lots of rework and wasted effort. The Pre-Release items are separated into two groups. The first group contains items 1-13. These are the must-have items that were part of the original 76-point checklist. The second group contains items 14-22. These are the advanced items added by other teams as they took the checklist and improved it. The advanced items are more

© Eric Passmore 2016
E. Passmore, *Migrating Large-Scale Services to the Cloud*,
DOI 10.1007/978-1-4842-1873-0_6

difficult to implement, so teams should work their way up to doing these items. Do not allow your team to get stuck while trying to do everything at once.

Pre-release items 1-13 (see Figure 6-1) cover the implicit needs of a large-scale global application. Most of the items on this list are *whats*. The following three items are *hows*:

- Item 1: Backward-compatible schema and API will enable rollback to last known good state without disrupting the client.

- Item 2: Versions for all assets in production enables rollforward and rollback for code and data.

- Item 13: Automation of pre-deployment processes enables the team to work at a faster speed and helps the team to close small, urgent tasks quickly.

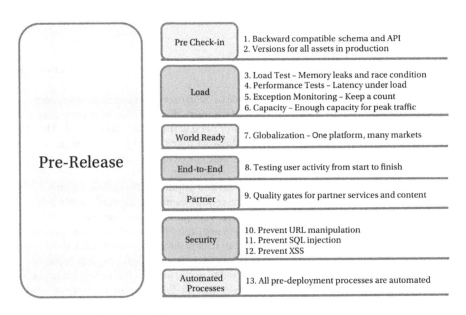

Figure 6-1. PreRlease Checklist part 1

The other items cover *whats*, and they provide general guidance. If the organization wants specific standards or outcomes, they need to develop a more exact and measurable set of standards. For example, an organization may want to issue a security stress test to evaluate compliance with the **Security** group (items 10, 11, and 12).

The **Pre Check-in** group ensures the right structure for services. Backward-compatible schemas need to be designed as part of the service. With each revision of the schema the team needs to make sure the promise of backward compatibility is maintained. In addition, having all of the assets in version management requires that configuration files, images, videos, JavaScript, and CSS are managed to store a history of changes and recover previous versions.

The **Load** group lists the key measurements to track during a stress test. Running a service at peak load can expose new bugs. The four measures listed in this section will detect the bugs. These measures may not help diagnose the problems, and additional data may be needed to fix the problem.

The **World Ready** group ensures that market-specific requirements are met. Some markets, like those using Hebrew, read right-to-left and have a different layout. The application needs to handle market-specific user interface customizations like right-to-left, left-to-right, and top-to-bottom layouts. In addition, there may be market-specific user telemetry requirements to integrate with region-specific market data providers.

The **End-to-End** group asks teams to create automated scenario tests that walk through a typical user interaction. Simulating a user login is not enough. A good scenario test will include a number of user interactions in a single session.

The **Partner** group creates a set of acceptance tests for services from other organizations. These acceptance tests detect when partner services changes create problems, and they may be run at regular intervals. It is best if these tests are automated to reduce the burden of setup and evaluation. It is recommended that teams work with their partners when developing these acceptance tests.

The **Security** group addresses a specific set of vulnerabilities. It is recommended to automate testing to provide immediate feedback and to run the tests periodically to ensure there are no regressions. Sharing examples of properly constructed code and encapsulating functionality into sharable packages is always a good practice.

The **Automation** group reminds us that all of the checklist items should be automated. Automation reduces the friction of setting up, executing, and evaluating work. By reducing this friction, tests may be run without human intervention and they may be run frequently. More automation leads to more frequent and stronger feedback loops.

Items 14-22 on the Pre-Release Checklist (see Figure 6-2) are advanced items. Several of these items require a significant engineering effort to build the capability needed to run the tests. Teams can develop these capabilities over time. One capability is image capture and comparison. The rise of mobile phones, tablets, and widescreen connected TVs have created a large range of screen sizes, resolutions, and screen dimensions. By automatically taking screen shots and comparing the images we can evaluate the user experience across devices.

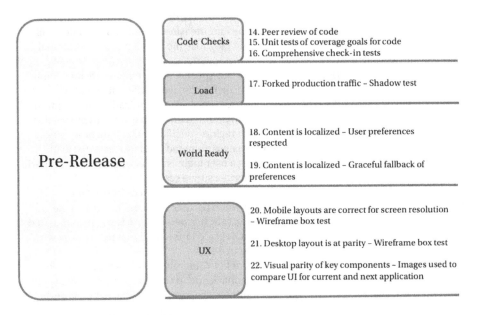

Figure 6-2. Pre-Release Checklist part 2

One type of test is an image comparison from release to release. Screenshots are captured as images. The images are compared and merged together into a single image with red and green coloring to highlight the changes. Most of the user experience remains the same from release to release. This test evaluates the stability in the user experience, and it neatly summarizes changes in the user experience for further review.

Another type of test is the wireframe box test. Again, screenshots are captured as images. The images are then processed to detect edges and obscure the content. The result of this processing is a set of boxes showing the layout of the page. This test ensures that the basic components of the page are correctly positioned. The header, navigation, main content area, and footer should all be aligned in their respective positons. In addition, the box test will capture popups and spamware that may appear.

The **Code-Check** group includes developer measurements of code quality. In many cases, this group includes gated tests that prevent the code from building a release candidate. The gated tests run after the code is compiled and they evaluate functional correctness; integration between services; security, privacy, and performance; and end-to-end scenarios. When the code passes the tests, a release candidate is built and put into a staging location or deployed directly into production. If the tests fail, the teams are alerted of the failures. The failures must be fixed before a release candidate may be built.

The **Load** group includes a *how*. This group asks the team to copy a small percentage of requests from production and reply to those requests in a pre-production environment. Replaying the copied traffic enables more accurate testing that reflects real-world scenarios. This is not an easy item to implement. The team needs to strip out any personally identifying information in the requests. In addition, it is best to sample across user sessions to get all of the requests from a single user interaction.

The **World Ready** group has two important items. The first is the requirement to give a user's explicit language and region setting the highest precedence. Often the language and region are automatically selected from a geo-lookup on the IP address or from the device's operating system preferences. If a user sets their region and language in the application, that preference should win out. The second requirement covers the case of a preferred language and market but no content to show. This requirement asks teams to fall back to another language-and-market combination without prompting the user.

The **UX** group covers the user experience. This group makes use of screenshots as images and image comparisons to ensure a quality experience. Compared to desktop PCs, mobile devices have a much different layout and structure to their applications. Performing a wireframe box test will ensure that critical components are on the devices. The additional test of comparing images between releases will make sure there are no regressions in the user experience.

Deployment Checklist

An automated release process eliminates the friction associated with pushing out software, and this enables faster and more frequent releases. Faster, more frequent releases are great when the quality of the release is good. When the quality of the release is poor, an automated release process enables faster and more frequent outages. Organizations often find they are able to automate releases only to find it is more painful as failures are amplified by the faster speed. Automating the deployment requires staying out of trouble while moving at a fast speed. The Deployment Checklist items identify the hidden risks and problems that can trip up good teams. Items 23-29 (see Figure 6-3) and items 30-33 (see Figure 6-4) are the expected must-have items for a large-scale, global cloud service. Items 34-37 (see Figure 6-5) cover flighting, an advanced topic.

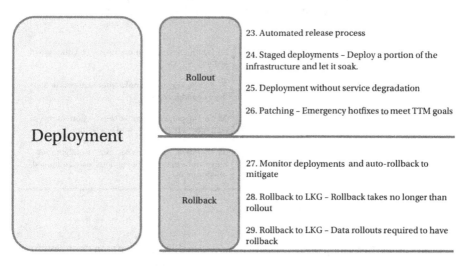

Figure 6-3. Deployment Checklist part 1

The **Rollout** group under the Deployment phase is all about staying out of trouble. Item 23 (automated release process) is the last part of a continuous integration cycle. It includes assembling the release candidate, along with the proper configuration file, and pushing the release out to all of the intended hosts. Item 24 (staged deployment) provides another opportunity to evaluate the release in production and find problems before those problems grow to unmanageable levels. A memory leak found after deploying to 10% of hosts is better than finding a memory leak after deploying to all of the hosts. Item 25 (deployment without service degradation) sets the bar for deployments. Users should not notice when a deployment is occurring. Item 26 (patching) asks teams to meet their Time to Mitigate (TTM) goals for fixes. If high-severity incidents have a target TTM of 90 minutes, and the mitigation requires a new release of software, then the release should take less than 90 minutes. Patching also implies a release could happen at any time in response to a live site incident.

If the **Rollout** group is about staying out of trouble, the **Rollback** group is about getting out of trouble. Item 28 (rollbacks to Last Know Good (LKG)) requires two things: the rollback process must be automated, and the version of the LKG release must be easily identified. Too often teams do not plan to roll back, and when they roll back, they do not know what version of the release to use. Item 29 (rollback data to LKG) reminds the team that data deployments are not immune from problems. An example of a data deployment is the image tiles generated by your favorite mapping service. Those tiles are generated in the background, and there is a mechanism for switching back to the old set of images tiles if something goes wrong.

Item 27 (automated rollback) is an obvious step and it needs be designed into the software from the start. Automated rollback requires monitoring and confidence in your alerts. When not done correctly, the automated rollback can incorrectly kick off and release the previous version of the software. Explaining to your boss that a false alarm triggered the entire web site to regress is not fun. Even more important, the rollback candidate needs to be ready to go. It is a good practice to store several versions of the application on a host. This will enable a fast switch between the current version and the LKG version.

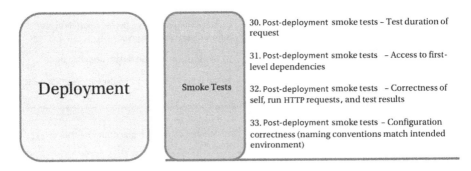

Figure 6-4. Deployment Checklist part 2

The **Smoke Test** group of checklist items prevents the most common deployment problems. Too often a fat-finger change to a vital configuration value will cause chaos when the release enters production. As an example, the web server on the US East Coast could be misconfigured to connect to a database in Hong Kong. Routing connections across the Pacific Ocean slows down the service response, and may even make the services unresponsive. Item 30 (test duration of the request) looks to find these global routing errors. Another common problem occurs when permissions change or a security certificate expires, preventing access to a much-needed service. Item 31 explicitly checks to make sure the new release can access critical dependencies. Every once in a while a completely broken release that does not work at all slips through testing and makes it out into production. As an example, a developer might hardcode a URL path that always points to the test environment. Item 32 does a very basic test of correctness on the new release. Finally, it is recommended that teams check to make sure configuration files use the production naming conventions. Item 33 (checking for production naming conventions) helps when the wrong configuration is in use. These problems really do happen, and running smoke tests on just one production host could save the team from putting out a completely broken release.

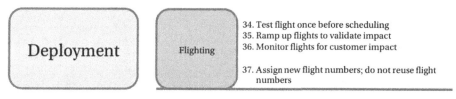

Figure 6-5. Deployment part 3

Flighting (see Figure 6-5) is the ability to direct a portion of traffic through different code pathways using the same release artifact. Flighting may be used to test any feature or set of features. Many developers love flighting because it enables experimentation and new code to run without requiring a release. The ability to light up a new feature set without building a release skips the automated testing and verifications that are built into the continuous integration cycle. The automated testing and verification is typically not aware of the flights and only the default pathway is tested. Therefore, a new flight has a good chance of exposing a feature set to production with little or no testing.

Flighting is an advanced capability and many engineers have the battle scars to prove it.

For this reason, item 34 (test flight once before scheduling) exists. Production should not be treated as a big lab, and teams are requested to test their new features set before going live. In addition, a flight could contain prototype or experimental work that is not ready for the full firehose of production traffic. In item 35, teams are asked to ramp up their usage over time instead of a big bang flight to everyone. In item 36, we ask teams to monitor the customer impact of the flighted experience. Looking at the business impact across all requests would bury the observations from the flighted experience in a sea of unrelated data. The observations need to be scoped to the flighted experience, and then all of the other requests need to be filtered out. Finally, item 37 (assign new flight numbers) ensures precision in the code pathway used. Using an old flight number may light up an old section of rusty code and revert the functionality of your service.

CHAPTER 7

■ ■ ■

Monitoring and Alerting Checklist

Business ends up being very dynamic and situational.

—Ben Horowitz

Not too long ago businesses had the opportunity to run on expensive hardware with multiple redundancies built in. Those same businesses were able to isolate services by creating specialized networks, racking the machines together, and providing dedicated power. These critical services could afford to go a long time between updates and patches. These services might have scheduled patch cycles and software updates that lagged releases by over 12 months.

In the public cloud, hardware is a commodity with redundancies purposely removed from the devices to better manage costs. Redundancy is created through networked computers, distributing the load across many hosts. In the public cloud, operating systems are updated constantly, with security patches lagging days or hours from release. In the public cloud, infrastructure is by default shared between multiple tenants. Compared to dedicated hardware, a public cloud host is more likely to be out of service. In the public cloud, increased hardware failures, more frequent patching, and throttling due to shared resources contribute to a lower availability per host. The public cloud has redundant hosts, self-healing, and the management tools to recover from failure with no loss of availability. This is a much more dynamic environment with a higher rate of change across a wider scope of concerns. Seeing the entire playing field requires a much broader, system-level view. When failures occur, a broad system view enables teams to categorize the problem, quantify the risks, and take the best corrective action.

In a dynamic environment, monitoring and alerting is so important. First, a broad array of concerns needs to be measured across a very large set of events. From those measurements, the noise needs to be filtered out. Across the datapoints, judgement is required to categorize the impact and nature of the event. Next, the event needs to be mapped to human-readable statements, and the information needs to be routed to the correct team.

© Eric Passmore 2016
E. Passmore, *Migrating Large-Scale Services to the Cloud*,
DOI 10.1007/978-1-4842-1873-0_7

The purpose of the Monitoring Checklist is to provide a concrete set of outcomes and steps to monitor the things that matter and to generate actionable alerts. The checklist comes from experience across both development and operations teams; as the checklist is shared, teams embrace the items with little modification.

The **Alerting** group (see Figure 7-1) is one of the most difficult areas to get right, and it covers eight items. Item 38 (actionable alerts) is the most important and requires a mind-set shift to get right. Engineers on the front lines receive alerts, and sometimes those alerts are received in the dead of night. Waking up in the early hours of the morning is hard. Shifting to understand why you have been woken up and then taking an action is even harder. Therefore, the best alerts help the on-duty team snap into mitigation. The goal of mitigation is to manage the impact by enabling services to operate at their highest possible business effectiveness.

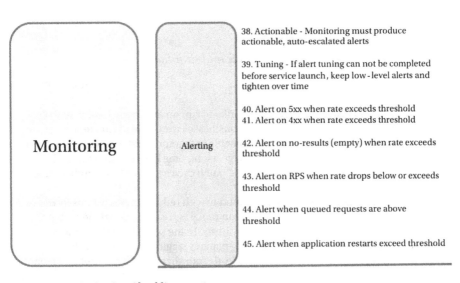

Figure 7-1. Monitoring Checklist part 1

Experience shows auto-generation of alerts is the most important factor in managing incidents. Human-escalated alerts have a more severe impact and longer impact duration. The discrepancy between human-escalated and auto-generated alerts grows as the organization gets larger. Navigating the organization is a very real challenge. For this reason, human-escalated alerts often work through a chain of people before reaching the right team. In addition, human escalations are communicated poorly, lacking both confidence in the severity of the incident and context on the nature of the incident. In a human-escalated alert, the receiving team will not be confident that there is a legitimate incident, and they will be less confident that they own the solution. Therefore, teams must first verify that an incident exists, and then investigate further to correctly route the incident. As a result, human escalations kick off a multi-pronged investigation of overall health before narrowing down to the specific context.

Auto-generated alerts are different. They are routed directly to the responsible team, and the auto-generated alert links to relevant information. In simple terms, auto-generated alerts are situationally aware.

When an incident does arise, corrective action is needed. The best alerts suggest what action to take as part of the alert and back up the suggestion with a diagnosis. When the alert is created, there is often enough information to both categorize the failure and suggest an action (see Table 7-1). The action could be a full mitigation to limit business impact, a link to a dashboard to investigate, or a checklist of additional steps to take. Teams creating alerts should put in the extra effort to think through the possible failures and suggest an action.

Table 7-1. *Examples of Good, Bad, and Ugly Alerts*

Alert Message	Example	Communication Method	Actionable	Auto-Escalate
Service is down	Bad	Call from boss	No, lacks context	No, direct call
Service is down	Bad	Auto-generated alert	No, lacks context	Yes, auto-generated
Index write failed (repeated 100 times)	Ugly	100 auto-generated alerts	No, lacks context	No, lacks escalation: all noise and no signal
Index service is down	Bad	Auto-generated alert	No, lacks action	Yes, auto-generated
Index service is down, and master node is in split mode	Bad	Auto-generated alert	No, lacks action	Yes, auto-generated
Index service in US-East is down, and US-West is taking over	Bad	Auto-generated alert	No, nothing to do	Yes, auto-generated
Index service in US-East is down, please initiate failover to US-West	Good	Auto-generated alert	Yes, suggested action	Yes, auto-generated
Index service in US-East is down, master node is in split mode, please initiate failover to US-West	Best	Auto-generated alert	Yes, suggested action with confidence in diagnosis	Yes, auto-generated

Item 39 (alert tuning) establishes the principle that alerts start off with a low severity unless there is evidence or reasonable concern of a high impact. Teams often create alerts with a high severity by default. That in turn causes all the alerts to go off during a major incident. When all the alerts go off, it creates a very noisy environment, and it is difficult to filter out the noise to take corrective action. Setting the alerts at a high severity seems to come from a fear of missing out on the one corner case that could cause an incident. Analysis of alerts and responses show that fear to be unfounded. Low-severity alerts do get attention, and last-mile synthetic tests act as a catch-all for service issues.

Items 41-45 alert from a time series of raw counters. Raw counters are important to mention because they collect a large number of datapoints and are therefore very precise. Typically the monitor will accumulate the total number of requests and the total number of errors each minute. A separate process looks over the last five minutes of counts and sums up the total number of errors. The total errors are divided by the sum of requests over the same period. This results in an error percentage. When the error percentage exceeds a target, an alert is raised.

Error Percentage = Total Errors / Total Requests

Success Percentage = (Total Requests − Total Errors) / Total Requests

---

Item 40 (alert on 5xx) looks for HTTP service errors. Teams may need to research the standard HTTP error codes to make sure they are correctly classifying service responses. The 5xx error codes are considered to be true errors. At MSN, we expect a 5xx error rate of 0.1% or less. Item 41 (alert on 4xx) looks for HTTP content errors. Teams may need to research the standard HTTP error codes to make sure they are correctly classifying service responses. The 4xx error codes are considered a lack of content or client error. At MSN, we expect a 4xx error rate of 1% or less. If your services do not use HTTP, a similar classification system with targeted error rates is recommended.

Item 42 (no response) counts the number of requests with an unusually small payload. Item 42 is often used to find times when an error response incorrectly provides a good response code. Item 43 creates an alert when there is an abnormal rate of service requests. An abnormally low or high rate may be a leading indicator of a capacity problem. Item 44 (queue requests) looks for backups occurring inside the service. Queuing is often an indicator of a bug in multi-threaded programing or a slowdown in downstream services. Item 45 (too many restarts) looks for service restarts, the most overused mitigation. Service restarts are not an effective long-term solution, and a high number of restarts requires investigation.

Items 46-54 (see Figure 7-2) cover two groups, Global Guidelines and Monitoring. The items in the **Global Guidelines** group come from experience managing global Internet properties. Item 47 (global coverage) is designed to catch big outages in small markets. When a small market has a major outage, the impact may not be noticeable when examining total error counts or traffic levels. For this reason, a big outage in a small market can go undetected for long periods of time. Item 48 (market coverage) highlights the need to cover unique market scenarios. For example, some markets need to use a customized and localized weather service. A global alert would not cover this market-specific customization, and a new monitor and alert need to be created. The bottom line is that markets require their own targeted set of monitors and alerts.

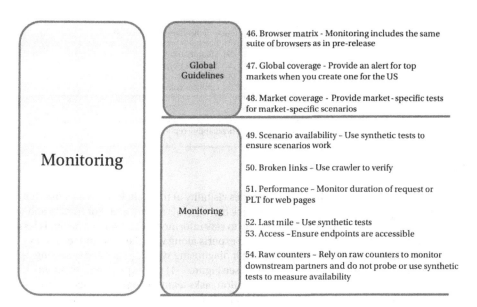

Figure 7-2. *Monitoring Checklist part 2*

The **Monitoring** group provides coverage across the entire platform and detects business-impacting incidents. Items 49-54 do not make up an exhaustive list. These six items are intended to highlight the often-missed monitors and ensure a very basic level of coverage. Item 49 (scenario availability) monitors the common user activity through probes inside the datacenter. Scenario availability is an end-to-end test, and a few tests will cover a broad surface area. Item 50 (broken link crawler) is another synthetic test that checks for bad links and can alert after repeated failures. The broken link crawler requires a working page, and it will find general service issues when the page does not load. Item 51 (performance) monitors how long the requests are taking to fulfill. Long requests indicate a problem downstream or a lack of capacity. Item 52 (last mile) is a special type of synthetic test executed outside the datacenter using third party services. The last mile tests will evaluate customer Internet connections and should include wireless carriers. Item 53 tests access to services from the outside world. Many times corporate users have the ability to access services but external customers are blocked by security policies. Item 54 (raw counters) looks for problems in downstream services; it is very precise due to the large number of collected datapoints.

Items 55-60 (see Figure 7-3) cover telemetry collection and availability reporting. The **Telemetry Collection** section includes measurements to aid in diagnosing problems. Items 55-58 measure basic compute and storage resources on a per-host level. Comparing these measurements across hosts is useful to find hosts in a bad or unresponsive state. Those hosts should be removed from taking live traffic. Item 59 (garbage collection) is important for computer languages that manage memory allocation. Poor choices in memory management and bugs can result in large garbage collection events that may cause a business impact.

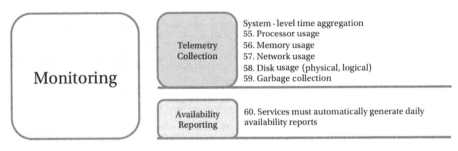

Figure 7-3. Monitoring Checklist part 3

The **Availability Reporting** group provides visibility at the team level. Teams use this visibility to drive corrective action when service health goals are not met. For leaders and partner teams, the daily report provides a way to stay informed. When service health is less than desired, teams need to be given access to experts along with the time and resources to address issues. Logs are a key component for diagnosing system issues and assessing improvements. The **Log** group has six points (see Figure 7-4) that explain how to retain better information. Item 61 (code instrumentation) asks teams to log stack traces from errors instead of supressing the error with a try and empty catch block. Stack traces enable the team to pinpoint the method and section of the code that is causing the problem. Item 62 (standardize) asks teams to log the critical details. For example, logs without timestamps make debugging an impossible task. Item 63 (correlation part 1) asks teams to include the *activity-id* with any internal logging. Item 64 (correlation part 2) asks teams to pass along the *activity-id* to downstream services so the requests may be tied together across the service stack. Item 65 (correlation part 3) asks teams to continue logging requests to correctly capture end-of-request details. Examples of end-of-request details include the duration of the request and the byte size of the request payload. Item 66 (log verbosity) explicitly asks teams to support different levels of logging at the request grain. Log verbosity enables precision debugging for requests with suspected bugs.

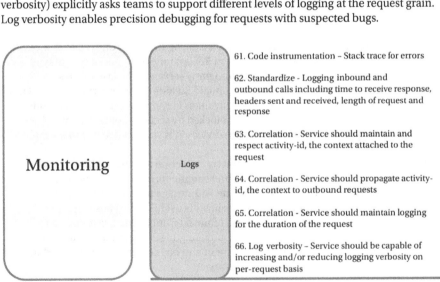

Figure 7-4. Monitoring Checklist part 4

The last item in the **Monitoring** group (see Figure 7-5) is an advanced item. Monitoring of mobile and tablet requests should always occur. Item 67 (multiple screens) requires native mobile applications to send back beacons with performance and debugging data. This includes crash reports. In addition, users of the mobile apps need to explicitly approve having the data sent back and collected. For native clients, this requires additional functionality and also requires users to install the new telemetry. For these reasons, monitoring multiple screens is an advanced topic and should be addressed over time.

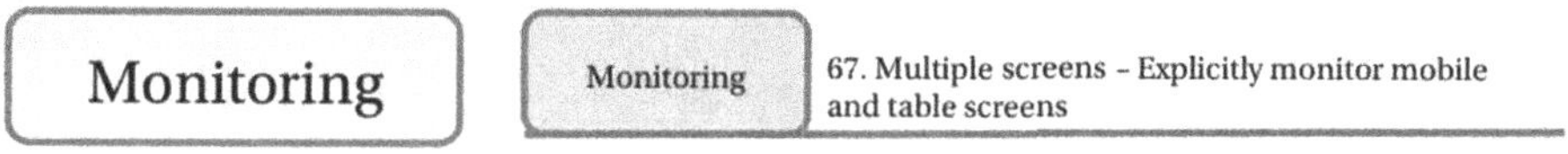

Monitoring	Monitoring	67. Multiple screens – Explicitly monitor mobile and table screens

Figure 7-5. *Monitoring Checklist part 5*

CHAPTER 8

Mitigation Checklist

I do not fix problems. I fix my thinking. Then problems fix themselves.

—Louise L. Hay

Things break, and services go down. Teams need to accept that outages will occur both in their own services and in services outside their control. In the public cloud, self-service tools enable a new degree of freedom. With this freedom comes additional responsibilities. Teams must develop services that are rugged and able to deal with failure. Team must develop the skills to respond effectively to incidents.

The Mitigation Checklist provides guidance in the following three areas:

- Tools needed to respond to incidents

- Skills needed to resolve incidents

- Critical features needed to make services robust

This checklist provides the must-have elements for each of these areas. It is not an exhaustive list. Implementing these checklist items will lessen the severity and frequency of business-impacting issues. Implementing these checklist items will not insulate the teams from failure. Therefore, the Mitigation Checklist should be seen as a good foundation that teams could build upon and advance with additional items.

The checklist items are agnostic of any roles and segregation of duties. The groupings are logical collections, and are not crafted to match development or operations roles. The groupings are intended to help readability and to make sense of the checklist at a glance. The items may be executed individually, and they are capable of standing on their own. For these reasons, teams should bring in experts from both software development and operations to collaborate and complete the work.

The **Diagnostics** group (see Figure 8-1) is about seeing and making sense of the information. Item 68 (live site visualization tools) is critical. Time series data shows the rate and degree of change over time. Having a historical perspective is important because it enables humans to quickly filter out normal variations and look for the exceptional changes. Having overlapping graphs from different sources helps to identify causes. For example, when comparing processing time across hundreds of hosts, the one host at 100% process utilization will immediate pop out. This bad child host should be removed from taking live traffic. Removing this one host will improve the overall service response time.

© Eric Passmore 2016
E. Passmore, *Migrating Large-Scale Services to the Cloud*,
DOI 10.1007/978-1-4842-1873-0_8

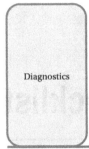

68. Live site visualization tools – Graphing time series data, overlaying the same data from different sources

69. Live site diagnostic tools – Specific tracing and debugging tooling

70. Stack debugging – Tracking tools that can pinpoint a break across services

71. Basic troubleshooting guides – Written steps to diagnose and mitigate alerts

Figure 8-1. *Mitigation Checklist part 1*

The key measures to graph are called out in the Monitoring and Deployment checklists. Item 69 is about making it easy to test hypotheses by generating requests and following the execution all the way through the stack. For example, take the case where there is a problem in the Netherlands. Infrastructure is shared across Europe, and none of the other markets are having issues. The team would fire up a tool to generate a request for the Netherlands and set the request to generate trace and debug information. The logs would then be returned for the generated Netherlands request and the teams could further investigate with the detailed information. Setting the trace and debug levels needs to be dynamic and at the request level, per checklist item 66. The tool is needed to correctly generate a targeted request, change the logging verbosity, and collect the logs.

Item 70 (stack debugging) describes the ability to query across the logs from multiple distinct services by a single *activity-id*. This enables teams to see broadly across all services. Item 71 (basic troubleshooting guides) is necessary in order to be prepared. When problems do happen, teams should be able to follow a guide to help them gather the information needed to make a decision. Good troubleshooting guides go beyond gathering information to suggest mitigating actions to take.

The next group is **Incident Management** (see Figure 8-2), and it was created to make sure teams are ready to handle outages with a big business impact. Item 72 (advanced troubleshooting guides) is an obvious first item. Even if the datacenter failover is completely automated, the troubleshooting guides should still exist. The process steps for doing a datacenter failover are important knowledge for the organization. The steps will be needed if and when the automation does not work. Item 73 (readiness) is an apt title for this item. It exists because teams often rise to the level of their training during a crisis. Item 74 (cross-team escalations) ensures that you have up-to-date contact information for other teams and experts. As organizations get larger, navigating the organization is an increasing challenge. Item 75 (fire drills) requires that teams practice to develop better teamwork and diagnostic skills. Item 76 (post-mortems) is an explicit ask that teams have a formal process to review and learn from incidents.

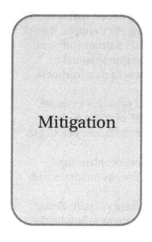

72. Advanced troubleshooting guides – Explicit written procedures with clear thresholds for datacenter failover and designed to meet TTM targets

73. Readiness – Complete online training for incident response

Incident Management

74. Cross-team escalations – Ensure your team has contact information and they know how to use that contact information for functional escalations

75. Fire drills – Drill teams to practice procedures

76. Postmortems – Complete reviews and resulting work items for high-impact incidents

Mitigation

Figure 8-2. Mitigation Checklist part 2

Figure 8-3 shows the **Business Continuity** checklist items. Item 77 (efficient manual failovers) becomes an explicit standard after teams missed their time-to-mitigate goals due to lengthy failover procedures. It would be great to have all failovers automated; however, this is not a reasonable expectation for prototype or experimental services. Item 78 (automated service failover) is a specific request that teams plan to handle coarse-grained service failure, and they automatically route around service failure. Interestingly, automated service failover does not require business parity. The new endpoint may be a degraded service with functionality turned off or removed. For example, if the US-East datacenter goes down, traffic may be automatically routed to the US-West datacenter with live weather and stock quotes turned off.

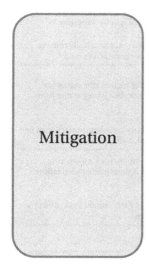
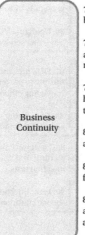

77. Efficient manual failovers – Manual failover can be completed within 30 minutes

78. Automated service failovers – Traffic is automatically routed to healthy service endpoints to maintain service

79. Automated partner failovers – Comprehensive health monitoring in place caches partner failure and triggers failover without human intervention.

Business Continuity

80. Data availability – All services must support active/active reads across datacenters

81. Sufficient capacity to handle load due to failovers (redundancy)

82. Disaster recovery plan – Teams must complete annual verification that services meet objectives for availability and data recovery

Mitigation

Figure 8-3. Mitigation Checklist part 3

Item 79 (automated partner failover) exists to manage partner issues. Teams need to work with partners to create a mutually acceptable failover plan. For example, if stock data is not available, the service might switch to another redundant partner endpoint.

Item 80 (data availability) sets the standard that data must be kept reasonable consistent for reads across datacenters. Data availability does not set a data freshness standard, and the data may be stale.

Item 81 (sufficient capacity) is required to handle failovers at peak. For example, when there are two datacenters, each must be able to handle 100% of traffic during peak. By meeting these targets there is enough capacity to handle the failure of a single datacenter.

Item 82 (disaster recovery plan) is an annual assessment to collect plans for datacenter failover and verify those plans by reviewing previous live site incidents with failovers.

Items 83-90 (see Figure 8-4) cover three groups: Service Resiliency, Traffic Spikes, and Fault Injection. The **Service Resiliency** group consists of four items to handle the most frequent incidents. Item 83 (auto-retry) asks services to expect temporary problems and recovery via a retry. It is a good policy to have a limited number of retries to prevent runaway, never-ending requests. Item 84 (set SLA downstream) reduces the confusion when dependancies act up. Having a quantifiable standard enables teams to manage expectations by establishing measures of health for dependant services. Item 85 (service degradation) makes it ok to degrade services rather than risk complete failure. Item 86 (configure VIP health) asks teams to make sure load balancers are configured to automatically removed bad hosts from service.

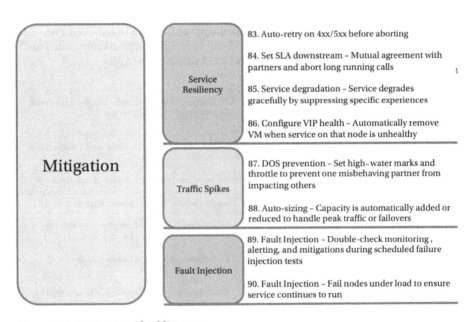

Figure 8-4. *Mitigation Checklist part 4*

Traffic Spikes and Denial of Service (Dos) attacks are common in the public cloud due to the open, publically facing endpoints. Hackers look for exploits open to the public. Sometimes DoS traffic is self-inflicted by runaway processes that spawn multiple requests. The **Traffic Spikes** group addresses these issues. Regardless of the source, throttling is a needed capability. In addition to DoS scenarios, teams are expected to utilize the self-service tools available in the public cloud to grow and shrink capacity to match demand. For example, if a new release of software adds 3D face detection on all images, then the image service will need additional capacity to support the new feature.

The **Fault Injection** group schedules failures to validate that monitoring, alerting, and service resiliency measures are in place. Item 89 (fault injection part 1) validates that monitoring, alerting, and mitigations are working. Item 90 (fault injection part 2) fails individual hosts in a service to validate service resiliency measures.

The last three items are advanced work items (see Figure 8-5). Item 91 (impact analysis tool) asks teams to develop tools to measure the number of users affected and the amount of revenue lost during an incident. These are difficult numbers to calculate because an outage may impact a narrow portion of functionality. Providing this data aligns the generals and foot soldiers to focus energy on fixing critical issues. Item 92 (post-mortem) for medium severity incidents asks teams to invest in learning. The post-mortem process can be lengthy and teams need support to perform these investigations. Item 93 is an extra-large engineering ask. It asks teams to make ensure that data is fresh and available regardless of failure. This is an advanced item because it is a costly endeavor that may take more than a year to complete.

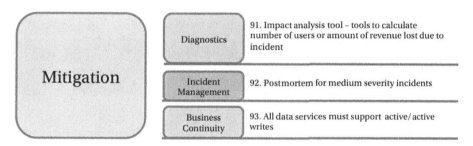

Figure 8-5. *Mitigation Checklist part 5*

Index

E. Passmore, *Migrating Large-Scale Services to the Cloud,*
DOI 10.1007/978-1-4842-1873-0

Get the eBook for only $5!

Why limit yourself?

Now you can take the weightless companion with you wherever you go and access your content on your PC, phone, tablet, or reader.

Since you've purchased this print book, we're happy to offer you the eBook in all 3 formats for just $5.

Convenient and fully searchable, the PDF version enables you to easily find and copy code—or perform examples by quickly toggling between instructions and applications. The MOBI format is ideal for your Kindle, while the ePUB can be utilized on a variety of mobile devices.

To learn more, go to www.apress.com/companion or contact support@apress.com.

Printed in the United States
By Bookmasters